A hugely readable testimon
love for Sco

Neil Doncaster SPFL

Following Sam is so much more than a tale of one fan and his dog. It's a life-affirming, inspirational and thought-provoking account of football and friendship. A complete and utter joy.

Michael McEwan Deputy Editor, *Bunkered*

Jon and Sam show us the depth of their passion and resilience, taking readers on a remarkable journey that's as inspiring as it is heartwarming. This book reveals their remarkable adventure, filled with challenges, triumphs, and the unbreakable bond between a man and his dog—a testament to courage, inclusivity, and the magic of the beautiful game.

Olivier Jarosz Chief Executive Officer, AccessibAll

We often say that football is the love supreme, but Jon's experiences with Sam show that the bond between dog and man is even greater. Poignant, honest and reaffirming in equal measure, a book to restore your love of both the beautiful game and humanity.

Kieran Maguire author and host, the Price of Football Podcast

Equally insightful and inspiring. Jon shows us that we can all achieve amazing things. From Dingwall to Dumfries, he dared to dream and his journey alongside Sam is a joyous adventure.

Hope Webb BBC Presenter and Reporter

A lovely, easy and heartwarming read and considering I'm not particularly a football fan, I really enjoyed the book.

Dr Michelle Selinger Principal Consultant

Going to the football is a pastime that many of us take for granted. But that's not the case for Jon (and Sam). And while their unique matchday experience is a challenge that most of us struggle to imagine, Jon's passion and enthusiasm for the game is as strong and infectious as anyone I've met.

The story of how he and Sam 'Conquered The 42' is an inspirational one, and is a tale of determination, of resilience, and of a love of the game shared by two very special characters.

Tino Host & Founder of The Celtic Exchange Podcast

This is more than the story of one man and his dog attending football matches. Jon (and Sam) provides an education in Scottish football with an insight into the challenges all fans, especially those with a disability, experience on match days. The love and passion for the beautiful game shines through.

Rob Palmer ESPN and Sky Sports football commentator

Jon follows Sam but over the past year so many of us have been following Jon. His passion for football is matched only by his belief that within it lies a family we can all be a member of across all corners of our country. His journey is one of positivity and community and ultimately one of love for both football and Sam.

Gavin Neate CEO and Founder, Welcome

FOLLOWING SAM

Jon and Sam's Journey Conquering the 42

JON ATTENBOROUGH

M^cNIDDER | &
GRACE

Published by McNidder & Grace
Jedburgh
Scotland
United Kingdom

www.mcnidderandgrace.com

First Published 2025
© Jon Attenborough

The author and publisher would like to thank all copyright holders for
permission to reproduce their work. Every effort has been made to obtain
necessary permission with reference to copyright material. The publisher
apologises if, inadvertently, any sources remain unacknowledged and will be
glad to be notified of any corrections that should be incorporated in future
editions of the book.

A catalogue record for this work is available from the British Library.

ISBN   9780857162830
eISBN 9780857162847

Cover design: Tabitha Palmer, Wales
Designer: JS Typesetting Ltd, Porthcawl, Wales
Printed and bound in the United Kingdom by Short Run Press, Exeter

For Mum and Dad,
who taught me the value of determination,
kindness and following my dreams.

Your love and guidance continue to inspire me
every day, even in your absence.

This journey, and this book, are for you.

CONTENTS

Prologue vii

Chapter 1 Life Before Sam 1

Chapter 2 The Scottish Professional Football
League 8

Chapter 3 Sam 15

Chapter 4 The First Five – Our Starting Line-Up ... 24

Chapter 5 Into Double Digits 36

Chapter 6 2020 48

Chapter 7 The Heart of the Journey 53

Chapter 8 Breaking Ground 65

Chapter 9 Disability Access in Football 78

Chapter 10 Start of the Second Half 86

Chapter 11 The Home Stretch 99

Chapter 12 Advocacy   114

Chapter 13 Closing in on the Finish   123

Chapter 14 Moments before the Final Whistle   137

Chapter 15 You'll Never Walk Alone   153

Chapter 16 Black & Tangerine   159

Chapter 17 Full Time – 42/42   166

Epilogue   176

The 42 Grounds   181

About the Author   183

Acknowledgements   184

Rest in Peace Sam   185

PROLOGUE

I never imagined that my life would be defined by football stadiums, much less by a dog. But here I am, reflecting on a journey that has taken me and my guide dog, Sam, to all 42 grounds in the Scottish Professional Football League (SPFL), a journey that would not have been possible without the incredible bond we share. It's funny how life can take unexpected turns, leading you to places and experiences you never thought possible.

Growing up, football was always there. I remember watching football with my dad and younger brother, listening to the roar of the crowd on the television, the sound of the ball being kicked around the pitch, and the excited commentary that made every match feel like a grand event. I couldn't see the game the same way others could, but I could feel it. I could sense the energy, the tension, the highs and lows of every match. It was something that brought me closer to others, even when I felt isolated by my visual impairment.

Living with limited vision wasn't always easy, but it was all I knew. I learned to navigate the world in my own way, relying on my other senses and developing an inner map of familiar places. But as I grew older, I realised that there were things I wanted to do, places I wanted to go, that were becoming increasingly difficult to manage on my own. I was born with two very rare eye conditions: *microphthalmia*, which literally means small eyes, and *coloboma*, which is a cleft in the structure of the eye. I have no sight at all in my right eye and limited vision in my left eye; I can read text if it is large enough and I hold it close to my face; but I can't make out anything in the distance or any fine details.

Meeting Sam was like discovering a new way to see the world. He wasn't just a guide dog; he was my partner and, soon enough, my best friend. Sam was trained to be my eyes, helping me navigate the challenges of everyday life with a calm and steady presence. But he was more than that, he had a personality that was impossible not to love. With his wagging tail and eager demeanour, Sam had a way of making everything seem possible.

When the idea of visiting all 42 SPFL football grounds first crossed my mind, it felt like a pipe dream, something that would be incredible to achieve but which was completely out of reach. After all, how could I, someone who once struggled with even the simplest of journeys, hope to travel across Scotland to some of the most remote football grounds? And yet, since being matched with Sam I had regained some self-confidence, and I realised that with him by my side, anything was possible.

The first step was convincing myself that this was something we could do. It wasn't just about the logistics – getting to each stadium, making sure everything was accessible. It was also about the mental and emotional commitment. This wasn't just a series of trips; it was a challenge that would test us in ways I could not predict. But the more I thought about it, the more I knew that this journey was something I needed to undertake, not just for myself but for everyone who has ever been told that they cannot do something because of their disability.

Our journey began with careful planning. I mapped out the football grounds, researching each one to understand the challenges. Some were in bustling cities, where crowds and noise would test Sam's focus. Others were in rural areas, where the terrain could be unpredictable and the facilities less than ideal. But no matter what obstacles lay ahead, I knew that Sam would guide me through them, just as he had guided me through so many other challenges.

As we set out on our journey, I was reminded of the first time I walked into a stadium with Sam. The sheer magnitude was overwhelming: the towering stands, the lush green pitch, the hum of anticipation that filled the air. I couldn't see it all, not in the way others could, but I felt it deeply. It was as though the stadium itself was alive, breathing with the collective energy of thousands of fans. I remember thinking how different this experience would have been without Sam. Before him, navigating such a space would have been overwhelming, perhaps even impossible. But with Sam by my side, I felt a sense of security, a reassurance that I could move forward with confidence.

Our first match together was a significant one, the Dundee derby at Tannadice Park! This was in September 2021, the first season that stadium restrictions had been lifted following the long and challenging Covid lockdowns. The anticipation was electric, not just because it was a derby match, but because it marked a return to something that had been missing from our lives for far too long. For me, this wasn't just another game; it was a homecoming, a rekindling of a passion that had been put on hold by the pandemic.

I am a proud Dundee United supporter, a devotion that took root in my teenage years. I vividly remember the first time I saw Dundee United live; it was a friendly match against none other than Pep Guardiola's Barcelona team in 2008. The atmosphere was electric, the excitement in the air palpable, and seeing players like Lionel Messi and Thierry Henry playing at Tannadice was surreal. That game wasn't just my introduction to live football; it was also the first match I attended with my younger brother, making it all the more memorable. The experience ignited a flame within me, a passion for football that would grow stronger with each passing year. I'm sure there are not many football fans who can say their first experience of a live game was watching the likes of Messi, Henry and Xavi in their prime!

Now, here I was, many years later, preparing to return to Tannadice for the first time since the pandemic, but this time there was something different, something special. This would be the first time I attended a match at Tannadice with my guide dog, Sam, and more importantly, it would be Sam's first football match. The excitement and nervousness I felt were intertwined, a mixture of anticipation for the game and curiosity about how Sam would react to the bustling, noisy environment of a football stadium.

In the week leading up to the derby, I decided to call the ticket office at Tannadice to inform them that I would be bringing along Sam. I wanted to ensure that everything would be in place for our visit, particularly given Sam's needs. I was connected with Moira Hughes, the club's Disability Access Officer, who turned out to be fantastic. Her kindness and professionalism put me at ease immediately. She not only helped me secure tickets but also went out of her way to ensure that Sam and I would be comfortable throughout the match.

Moira organised accessible seating for us, ensuring that there would be plenty of room for Sam to lie down and be comfortable. She understood that this wasn't just about watching a game; it was about making sure that both Sam and I could enjoy the experience without any unnecessary stress. Then, Moira asked if I would be interested in tuning into the audio-descriptive commentary. I had never heard of this service before, so she explained that it was a specialised commentary service designed for blind and visually impaired supporters. The commentators provide a detailed, play-by-play description of the action on the pitch, allowing those who can't see the game to follow along as if they're right there in the middle.

This offer intrigued me. As much as I loved the atmosphere of football, the cheers of the crowd, the chants echoing through the stadium, I had always missed out on the finer details of the game. The idea that I could experience the match more fully through this service was both exciting and a little overwhelming. I accepted the offer, eager to see how this new experience would enhance my understanding and enjoyment.

The day of the derby finally arrived, and as we approached Tannadice Park, I could feel the excitement building inside me. Sam trotted alongside me, his tail wagging enthusiastically, seemingly feeding off the energy of the crowd around us. Stepping into the stadium was like stepping into another world. The noise, the sea of black and tangerine, the sheer energy of the crowd, was overwhelming, but in the best possible way. As we found our seats, I couldn't help but feel a sense of pride. Not just in my team, but in the journey that had brought us here. The journey that had turned a daunting challenge into an achievable goal, all thanks to the unwavering bond between a man and his dog.

And so, as the players took to the pitch and the first whistle blew, I tuned into the audio-descriptive commentary for the first time. The detailed narration brought the game to life in a way I had never before experienced. Every pass, every tackle, every shot on goal was described with such clarity that I felt that I could see the action unfolding before me. Sam lay calmly at my feet, his presence a comforting constant as I immersed myself in the game.

That day, the Dundee derby wasn't just another match; it was a milestone, a testament to the journey Sam and I would embark upon together. It was the beginning of a new chapter, one where football, once a distant passion, became an accessible and exhilarating experience once again.

Chapter 1
LIFE BEFORE SAM

I grew up in Newburgh, a small village nestled in the heart of North East Fife. Newburgh is the kind of place where time feels like it moves just a bit slower, where the days are long and the nights are quiet. The village sits on the south bank of the River Tay, and from almost anywhere, you can catch a glimpse of the water as it stretches towards the horizon.

Newburgh is one of those villages where everyone knows each other. It's a comforting place, where you can't walk down the street without someone offering a warm smile or a friendly hello. I remember how the cobbled paths echoed with the sound of familiar voices, how neighbours chatted for what seemed like hours outside their front gates. There was a sense of community that wrapped around you like a warm blanket on a cold day.

The village also boasts a well-supported non-league football club, Newburgh, previously known as Newburgh Juniors. The team currently plays in the East of Scotland League Third Division, but for us locals, it always felt like they were playing in the big leagues. On match days, East Shore Park came alive with excitement. The smell of freshly cut grass mingled with the scent of pies from the concession stand, and the air buzzed with the chatter of loyal fans. I often found myself heading down to the park with my younger brother or a few friends from school. We stood there, huddled in our jackets, as we watched the game unfold, our breath visible in the cool air.

Newburgh is also the hometown of Stevie May, a name that now echoes in the stands of St Johnstone's McDiarmid Park. But back then, Stevie was just another kid from the village, albeit a kid with extraordinary talent. He was in my brother's class at school, so I got to know him a bit. After school, we often gathered at the park for a kickabout, and there was always a sense of anticipation when Stevie showed up. Even then, we all knew that he was something special. When we picked sides, everyone wanted Stevie on their team, and for good reason: he could outplay us all without breaking a sweat.

I remember watching him in awe, knowing that while we were just playing for fun, Stevie was on a different path. His passion for the game was evident in every move he made, every shot he took. It was as if the ball was an extension of him, something he controlled with effortless precision. Every boy dreams of becoming a football star, but for Stevie, it was never just a dream, it was destiny. We could all see that his future was bright, that he was meant for something greater. And now, seeing him play professionally, I can't help but feel a swell of pride for the boy who grew up kicking a ball around in our little village.

Being born with a significant visual impairment brought its own set of challenges, particularly when it came time to start school. The world of education is challenging enough for any child, but for me, it required an additional layer of support – support that wasn't always readily available. My dad became my biggest advocate, taking on the role of a fierce protector and tireless campaigner to ensure I had access to the resources and assistance I needed.

Looking back now, I realise just how much my parents, especially my dad, had to fight. At the time, I had no idea of the struggles happening behind the scenes. I didn't know about the meetings, the letters, the phone calls, all the countless hours my dad spent making sure I had what I needed to thrive. It wasn't until I was much older that I began to understand the extent of his efforts. He went above and beyond to make sure I could start life on equal terms with my peers, to make sure that my visual impairment wasn't a barrier to my education and development.

In Scotland, we have a system of support for visually impaired students known as Qualified Teachers of Visual Impairment (QTVIs). These are specialised educators trained to assist visually impaired pupils in both primary and secondary school. I was fortunate to be supported by some fantastic QTVIs throughout my educational journey. They weren't just there to help me with my studies; they were lifelines, helping me navigate a world that wasn't always designed with people like me in mind. They worked tirelessly to adapt materials, to ensure that I could participate fully in class, and to help me build the skills I needed to succeed – not just academically, but in life.

Leaving school was a significant transition for me, and one I was ready to embrace thanks to the solid foundation I had been given. My next step was college in Perth, where I decided to study music, an area where I felt I could express myself without limitations. Music had always been a passion of mine, a way to connect with the world in a way that words sometimes couldn't. I completed my Higher National Certificate (HNC) in Music, which was a huge achievement for me and a testament to the hard work I'd put in.

After college, my life was hit with one of its most devastating blows. My dad, at just 50 years old, was diagnosed with lung cancer. The news felt like a punch to the gut, something so unreal that it was hard to believe. My dad had always been a hard-working man, running his own painting and decorating business with a pride that defined him. He poured his heart and soul into his work, and the idea that he would have to give it up was unimaginable. But cancer doesn't care about your plans or your passions.

I remember vividly one day when his phone rang and someone on the other end asked if he could come and do some work for them. My dad, who always took such pride in his work, had to tell them that he was no longer in business. I could see the pain in his eyes, the reality of his illness hitting him in that moment. It wasn't just the work he was losing; it was a part of his identity. The sadness in his voice as he explained that he was too ill to continue was heart-wrenching. It was one of the first moments that the gravity of his illness hit home for me.

When he was given a terminal diagnosis, the doctors estimated he had roughly six to nine months to live. I'll never forget the day he and Mum came back from the hospital with the news. They gathered my younger brother, sister and me around the dinner table. My dad, who had always been the strong, stoic figure in my life, struggled to get the words out. When he finally told us that his time was limited, I saw something I had never seen before: my dad, the man who never showed vulnerability, broke down in tears.

Seeing him cry was like seeing a pillar crumble. My heart shattered. I wanted so badly to cry with him, to let the pain out right there at the table, but something inside me stopped. I felt like I had to be strong for my mum, for my brother and sister. So I held it in, forcing myself to stay composed, even though everything inside me was falling apart. As soon as I could, I retreated to my bedroom, where I finally let the tears flow freely. I cried for my dad, for our family, for the unfairness of it all.

My dad's illness progressed quickly, far quicker than any of us could have anticipated. The months that followed were a blur of hospital visits, moments of fleeting hope and the ever-present shadow of what was to come. He fought as hard as he could, but cancer is a relentless foe. On 8 November 2010, just six months after his diagnosis, my dad passed away at the age of 51.

Losing him felt like losing a part of myself. He had been more than just my dad; he was my role model, the person who had fought so hard to give me the best start in life. His absence left a void that I knew would never be filled. Even now, the memory of those final months is both painful and precious, a reminder of the love we shared and the strength of a man who, even in his final days, taught me so much about courage and resilience.

After he passed away, I found myself at a crossroads, trying to figure out the next chapter of my life. That's when I saw an opportunity to apply for a position as a Community Coach at St Johnstone in Perth. Football had always been a love of mine, and the idea of coaching, of being part of the game in a new way, was incredibly exciting. I had already participated in a couple of the Scottish Football Association (SFA) Community Coaching courses in the local area during my time at college, so when the position at St Johnstone opened up, I jumped at the chance.

The instructor on the course was Atholl Henderson, a former footballer himself and now head of the community coaching department. When I went for my interview, it was a stroke of luck that Atholl and I had already crossed paths during the coaching courses. That connection, combined with my passion and enthusiasm for the role, helped me secure the position. It was only a temporary job, but my time at St Johnstone was invaluable. I learned about more than football coaching; I learned about leadership, teamwork and resilience. These were lessons that extended far beyond the pitch and have stayed with me ever since.

However, my temporary position came to an end, and for the first time since leaving school, I found myself unemployed. It was a strange and unsettling feeling, but life has a funny way of opening new doors when you least expect. Not long after, I came across an advertisement for a trainee finance position at RNIB Scotland in Edinburgh. I'll admit, finance wasn't an area where I had any experience, and to be honest, I wasn't particularly good at maths during school. In fact, it was one of my least favourite subjects! But something about the opportunity intrigued me, and I decided to give it a shot.

To my surprise, I got the job. The role was a steep learning curve, but I threw myself into it. Over time, I discovered I was actually quite good at accountancy! The world of numbers, which had once seemed so daunting, started to make sense, and I found myself enjoying the challenges that came with the job. It was a complete turnaround from my school days, and if you had told me back then that I would come to love working in finance, I would have laughed in disbelief!

I spent over five years at RNIB, and it was a rewarding time. I worked alongside some amazing people, and I still keep in touch with many today. They weren't just colleagues; they were mentors, friends and supporters who helped me grow, both professionally and personally. My time at RNIB wasn't just about learning the ins and outs of finance; it was about building confidence, honing my skills and discovering a new path.

Eventually, I decided to further my qualifications in accountancy. This was a decision driven by a desire to keep pushing myself, to keep growing and learning. So I left RNIB to pursue formal accountancy qualifications, with the goal of advancing my career in a field that had unexpectedly become a passion.

Looking back, my journey has been one of overcoming challenges, embracing new opportunities and finding my way in a world that wasn't always designed for someone with a visual impairment. But with the unwavering support of my family, the incredible educators who believed in me, and the chance encounters that led me down new paths, I've been able to carve out a life that I'm proud of, a life where my visual impairment isn't a limitation but just one part of the story.

Chapter 2
THE SCOTTISH PROFESSIONAL FOOTBALL LEAGUE

A total of 963 days. That's how long it took Sam and I to visit all 42 SPFL grounds to watch a game. Nearly three years of planning, travelling and exploring every corner of Scotland, from bustling cities to remote towns, all driven by my passion for football. We travelled to every single game using public transport too, mostly trains but also buses and sometimes taxis where needed. We journeyed through all sorts of weather and landscapes, from the brisk winds sweeping across the northern reaches of Elgin and Dingwall to the milder, often rainy climate of Dumfries and Annan in the south. Every trip carried its own unique set of experiences. We found ourselves on a bus driving along the rugged coastlines of the northeast to Peterhead, where the North Sea's presence was undeniable, and also down to Stranraer in the south-west, a town shaped by its proximity to Ireland across the Irish Sea. Actually, when we did travel to Stranraer, on 22 June 2024, it was for a preseason friendly game at Stair Park between Stranraer and Larne, a team from Northern Ireland. It took the Larne team less time to travel on the ferry across to Stranraer for the game and back again afterwards than it did for myself and Sam to travel to the game and back home again! That's how remote Stranraer is as a town.

It was not just the destinations but the people we met along the way, the local fans whose genuine love for their teams rivalled any top-tier European club, and the smaller communities where match days were the beating heart of local culture. We immersed ourselves in the traditions, from pies at half-time to the passionate singing that reverberated through the stands, each ground offering its own unique slice of Scottish football life.

Each of these clubs represents the hope and determination that exists within the lower leagues, where dreams of trophies are nurtured, and where, against the odds, some of those dreams are realised. Witnessing these stories unfold across 42 grounds was more than just a journey; it was a testament to the enduring spirit of Scottish football.

The Scottish Professional Football League, known simply as the SPFL, is the pinnacle of Scottish football, overseeing the nation's most elite football competitions. It was officially formed in 2013, a relatively recent development in the grand history of Scottish football, by merging the Scottish Premier League (SPL) and the Scottish Football League (SFL). This merger was designed to streamline the professional game in Scotland, creating a more unified structure and addressing financial and organisational challenges that had plagued the sport in the years leading up to its formation.

Before the SPFL, the SPL had operated as the top tier of Scottish football since its establishment in 1998 after breaking away from the SFL, which had run the leagues since 1890. This split was driven by the desire of the top clubs to maximise television revenue, a move that mirrored similar changes in other European countries. However, the split also led to a fragmented system, and the SPL and SFL were sometimes pulling in different directions. The formation of the SPFL was seen as a necessary step to bring all professional clubs under one umbrella, fostering a more cohesive and competitive football environment.

The SPFL's structure, comprising the Premiership, Championship, League One and League Two, provides a clear and competitive framework for clubs at various levels of football. The league system is designed to ensure that clubs can move up or down based on their performance, and promotion and relegation battles add to the excitement each season. At the top, the Premiership is home to Scotland's most prestigious clubs, including Celtic and Rangers, whose historic rivalry – known as the Old Firm or, more recently, the Glasgow Derby depending on who you ask – is one of the most famous and intense in world football. This rivalry has dominated Scottish football for over a century, and both clubs have amassed a staggering number of league titles and trophies between them.

Beneath the Premiership, the Championship is often where the drama intensifies. Clubs here are either striving to reach the top tier or fighting to avoid dropping into League One, creating a fiercely competitive environment. The Championship is known for being unpredictable; it's not uncommon for a team to surge from the middle of the table to clinch a promotion spot or, conversely, to slip into the relegation zone. This level of unpredictability makes the Championship one of the most exciting leagues to follow in Scotland, where every match can have significant implications for the final standings.

League One and League Two, while featuring smaller clubs, are no less passionate. These leagues are where local pride and community spirit shine brightest. The clubs in these divisions may not have the financial resources or fan bases of their Premiership counterparts, but what they lack in size, they make up for in heart and determination. For many of these clubs, the goal is not just survival but to build momentum and gradually climb the league system – with the dream of one day reaching the higher echelons of Scottish football.

One of the key elements of the SPFL's appeal is the promotion and relegation system. At the end of each season, the bottom club in the Premiership faces automatic relegation to the Championship, while the second-bottom club must navigate a play-off against teams from the Championship to retain their place in the top division. Similarly, promotion from the Championship to the Premiership is awarded to the league champions, while teams finishing in the play-offs compete for the second promotion place. This system creates a thrilling end to each season as multiple clubs battle for their futures in every division.

The SPFL covers the top 42 clubs, but the structure below is just as vital to the health of Scottish football. The Highland and Lowland leagues, representing the north and south of Scotland respectively, are the highest levels of non-league football. They play a crucial role in the football pyramid, acting as a bridge between the professional and amateur games. Clubs in these leagues may not enjoy the same level of attention or resources as those in the SPFL, but they are an integral part of the fabric of Scottish football, often serving as the heart of their local communities.

The promotion process from these leagues into the SPFL is one of the most gruelling and talked-about aspects of the Scottish football pyramid. The winners of the Highland and Lowland leagues face off in a play-off, and the victor then challenges the bottom-placed team in League Two for a spot in the SPFL. This set-up, while controversial, adds a layer of drama and intensity to the end of each season as clubs from different tiers clash with everything on the line. It's a system that has been both praised for its excitement and criticised for its difficulty, but it undeniably adds to the rich tapestry of Scottish football.

Several clubs have managed, despite the challenges, to break through this barrier in recent years. Cove Rangers, for example, have been a beacon of success since gaining promotion to the SPFL. After winning the Highland League and successfully navigating the play-offs, they quickly made their mark by securing promotion to League One and even reaching the Championship, albeit briefly. Their rise has been a source of inspiration for other non-league clubs, demonstrating that with the right blend of talent, management and community support, anything is possible in Scottish football.

Kelty Hearts is another club that has embraced the challenge of moving up through the pyramid. After dominating the Lowland League, they earned their place in the SPFL and have continued to push upwards, achieving promotion to League One after just a short stint in League Two. Their rapid ascent through the divisions is a testament to their ambition and the quality of their football, proving that the pyramid system, despite its hurdles, allows for new blood to rise through the ranks and challenge the established order.

Bonnyrigg Rose, though newer to the SPFL, has also shown that clubs from the Highland and Lowland leagues can not only survive but thrive in professional football. By maintaining their status in League Two, they have set a foundation for future success, with aspirations to continue their climb up the divisions. For fans of these clubs, the journey through the football pyramid is not just about the destination, but about the experiences and memories made along the way – the big victories, the nail-biting play-offs and the sheer joy of defying the odds.

One of the fun facts about the SPFL is that it is home to some of the oldest football clubs in the world. Queen's Park, for instance, is Scotland's oldest football club, founded in 1867. Known as The Spiders, they played a significant role in the development of modern football, including being one of the first clubs to adopt passing as a key tactic, a revolutionary concept at the time. Queen's Park spent much of their history as an amateur club, and turned professional only in 2019. They have been climbing the SPFL ladder ever since, recently earning promotion to the Championship.

The SPFL is also notable for its geographical diversity. Unlike many other leagues that are concentrated in urban areas, the SPFL covers a wide range of locations, from the Highlands in the north to the Borders in the south, and from the remote towns to the bustling central belt. This diversity means that each away trip can feel like a journey to a different world, with varying landscapes, cultures and footballing traditions.

One of the quirkiest aspects of the Scottish football pyramid is the location of Dingwall, home to Ross County. Dingwall is one of the smallest towns to host a top-flight football team, with a population of just over 5,000. Despite this, Ross County has established itself as a competitive force in the Premiership, even winning the Scottish League Cup in 2016. Their success is a testament to the unique charm of Scottish football, where even the smallest communities can produce teams capable of competing at the highest level. The capacity of Ross County's stadium even exceeds the population of the town!

As I reflected on the journey Sam and I have made to all 42 SPFL grounds, I realised that Scottish football is more than just a game; it's a way of life. Each ground we visited has its own story, its own heroes and its own place in the grand narrative of Scottish football. From the towering stands of Celtic Park to the intimate surroundings of Gayfield Park in Arbroath, we witnessed the full spectrum of what makes Scottish football special. It's a sport deeply intertwined with the identity of the nation, and one that continues to captivate and inspire fans from all walks of life.

Chapter 3
SAM

Around 2015 the sight in my left eye began to deteriorate. I first started to become aware of this when walking to work between Edinburgh Waverley station and the offices of RNIB Scotland, on Hillside Crescent. On several occasions I bumped into someone, or brushed against a lamppost. What followed was multiple hospital appointments over the next few years, but my immediate problem was my mobility.

Working for RNIB at the time was fortunate, because they were able to provide me with a long cane and helped organise training with a mobility instructor. Until this point I was just about managing to get around without a mobility aid, and to be honest I wasn't thrilled. In fact, I hated my long cane, not least because I never really had great long cane skills. Even to this day, I still hate using my cane to get about. I remember talking about this with Mum, who suggested I should consider a guide dog. I love dogs, and we had always had pet dogs when we were growing up, so I was used to them and knew about the responsibilities that came with being a dog owner. I decided to give Guide Dogs a call.

The Guide Dogs for the Blind Association is more than just a charity; it is a beacon of hope and independence for countless individuals, myself included. In a world that can often feel overwhelming and isolating, this charity has become one of the UK's most recognisable and respected organisations. Its impact on my life has been nothing short of transformative, allowing me to reclaim my confidence and live life on my own terms without the constant need to rely on others.

My journey with guide dogs began with Zorba, a magnificent Golden Labrador Retriever cross. Zorba was more than just a dog; he was my partner, my lifeline. I remember our first meeting vividly, when I was struck by his size and strength. He was a big lad, more muscular than I had expected for a Labrador, with a presence that exuded both power and calm. From that moment, I knew that Zorba would be a steady and reliable companion, someone I could trust to navigate the complexities of life.

Zorba and I quickly formed a bond, albeit unique. He wasn't the most affectionate dog: if I tried to put my arm around him for a hug, he often pulled away, not out of anxiety but because he simply wasn't that kind of dog. He had his own way of showing affection, and our connection was built on mutual respect and understanding rather than overt displays of love. Zorba's personality was as strong as his physique, and he took his work seriously, guiding me through the busy streets of Edinburgh. His calm and steady demeanour put me at ease, and with Zorba by my side, I felt invincible.

When we were first matched, I worked at RNIB Scotland, and he accompanied me on the train to work. The hustle and bustle of the train station, the crowded platforms, the noise – it didn't faze him in the slightest. He was a diligent worker, always focused on the task, ensuring that I reached my destination safely. It was during these commutes that I truly appreciated the training and dedication that goes into training a guide dog. Zorba was more than just a helper; he was an extension of myself.

We were partnered in 2016, and for nearly two years, Zorba was my constant companion. But our time together was cut short. In early 2018, Zorba was attacked by another dog, a moment that changed everything. The attack left him deeply traumatised, and particularly fearful of smaller dogs. The support from the Guide Dogs Association was unwavering, and Zorba was offered retraining and rehabilitation to help him overcome his fears. But the trauma had taken root, and Zorba could no longer work as a guide dog. His early retirement was a devastating blow, to us both.

Losing Zorba felt like losing a part of myself. After being matched with him, I had worked hard to rebuild my confidence and suddenly, I found myself back on the waiting list, forced to rely on a long cane that I had never fully embraced. It felt inadequate by comparison to the partnership I had shared with Zorba, and I struggled to regain my sense of independence. The waiting period was filled with uncertainty and longing, but I knew I had to be patient. The bond between a guide dog and their owner is not something that can be rushed or replicated easily; it is a connection built on trust, respect and understanding.

Guide dogs undergo extensive and highly specialised training to prepare them for the vital role they play in the lives of those with visual impairments. The process begins when they are just six weeks old, placed in the care of volunteer Puppy Raisers who provide them with a loving home and the socialisation they need to thrive. These early months are crucial, as the puppies are introduced to a variety of environments: busy towns and cities, public transportation and other everyday situations they will encounter as guide dogs. This exposure helps them become well-rounded, confident dogs, ready to take on the challenges of guiding a visually impaired person.

When the puppies reach around 12 months of age, they move on to Guide Dog School, where their formal training begins. It is here that they are introduced to the harness, the symbol of their new role as a guide dog. The training at this stage is intense, focusing on the development of their basic guiding skills, learning to navigate obstacles, stop at kerbs and follow commands that will keep their handler safe. The process is rigorous and not every dog is suited for the work, but those who make it through go on to change lives in ways that are difficult to quantify.

The training is conducted at Regional Centres throughout the UK, each one dedicated to training the best guide dogs possible. In Scotland, the Regional Centre is in Forfar, a place that has become synonymous with hope and new beginnings for many – and, of course, home of the Forfar bridies (if you know, you know)! The dog trainers there are experts in their field, working tirelessly to ensure that each dog is matched with the right person, creating partnerships that can last a lifetime.

The dogs spend 5–6 months completing their foundational training at the Regional Centres, learning the essential skills of guiding. Then they progress to advanced training. This stage is critical, marking the transition from a dog who is highly trained to a guide dog whose assistance is life-changing. During this period, a Guide Dog Mobility

Specialist (GDMS) takes the lead, working closely with the dog to fine-tune their abilities, ensuring that they can handle the specific needs of a future owner. It's a delicate process, one that requires both expertise and an innate understanding of the dog's temperament, abilities and potential.

The role of the GDMS is multifaceted. Not only do they perfect the dog's guiding skills, but they also play a crucial part in the matching process, perhaps the most pivotal moment in the journey of a guide dog. Matching a dog with a client on the waiting list is more than just pairing up a dog with someone who needs assistance; it's about finding the right partner for life. This bond between the dog and its owner is built on trust, mutual respect and an unspoken connection that goes beyond commands and obedience. The GDMS must consider the dog's personality, energy level and working style and how these attributes align with the lifestyle, pace and needs of the person who will rely on the dog every day. It's not just about ensuring the dog can perform tasks, it's about creating a harmonious relationship where both dog and handler can thrive together.

When a match is found, it's a moment of hope and anticipation. For the person on the waiting list, it may mark the beginning of a new chapter, one filled with the promise of regained independence and the freedom to move through the world with confidence. But before this partnership can truly begin, there is one more crucial step: the training class.

The training class is an intensive, immersive experience that spans about four weeks. It's designed to equip the new guide dog owner with all the knowledge and skills they need to work effectively with their dog. The first two weeks are particularly challenging, as they involve residential training away from home. During this time, the person and their guide dog are immersed in a structured environment where they can focus entirely on building their relationship and mastering the tasks that will become part of their daily routine. It's a time of deep learning, where every moment is dedicated to understanding how to communicate with the dog, learning the commands and getting accustomed to following the subtle movements of the harness.

The emotional journey during these two weeks is intense. For many, it's the first time they've had to fully rely on another being for their mobility and safety, and this can be both empowering and daunting. There's a learning curve, moments of triumph when a command is successfully executed, and moments of frustration when things don't go as smoothly. But through it all, the bond between the person and their guide dog begins to take shape. The residential training is a safe space for making mistakes, learning from them and building the trust that is so essential in a guide dog partnership.

After the initial two weeks of training, the process shifts to the comfort and familiarity of the person's home. The next two weeks are spent learning to navigate regular routes such as going to work and visiting the local shops, taking the same paths that will become part of the dog's daily routine. This home-based training is crucial because it allows the guide dog and owner to adapt to the specific environment where they will be working together. It's about making sure the dog can guide effectively in real-world scenarios, where the challenges and obstacles are familiar but still require precision and confidence.

The emotional impact of this training phase cannot be overstated. For the person, it's often a time of reawakening, rediscovering the independence that may have been lost or diminished before having a guide dog. The dog becomes more than just a helper; they become a partner, a source of strength and a constant companion. The person learns to trust again, not just in the dog but in their own ability to navigate the world with this new ally by their side.

The matching process, training and final homecoming of a guide dog represent a journey of hope, resilience and new-found freedom. The relationship between a guide dog and their owner is unique, built on a foundation of mutual respect and unwavering trust. It's a partnership that not only changes the life of the person who gains independence but also allows the dog to fulfil its purpose in a profound way.

Guide Dogs for the Blind has a long history of creating these partnerships. Since its founding in 1931, the organisation has been committed to helping those with visual impairments lead more independent lives. The work they do goes beyond training dogs; it's about fostering relationships that empower individuals, giving them the confidence to pursue their goals and dreams with a loyal companion by their side.

After Zorba's retirement, I was very fortunate to be matched quite quickly with Sam, who has continued to change my life in profound ways. Sam, like Zorba, is a Golden Labrador Retriever cross, and from the moment we were paired, I knew we were a perfect match. Sam brought with him a new sense of energy and enthusiasm, rekindling the confidence that had wavered after Zorba's enforced retirement. Together, we've continued to explore the world, Sam guiding me through new challenges and experiences, always by my side and always ready to lead the way. Sam, unlike Zorba, is very affectionate! He loves cuddles, loves attention and loves being around people.

The journey with a guide dog is one of growth and mutual reliance. It's about learning to let go of fear and embracing the independence that comes from having a trusted companion by your side. For those of us who rely on guide dogs, these animals are more than just pets, they are lifelines, providing us with the freedom to live our lives fully and independently.

Sam is more than just a dog; he's the embodiment of love and loyalty. From the moment you see him, a wave of warmth and affection engulfs you, making it impossible not to fall for his gentle spirit. The instant our eyes meet, his tail begins wagging furiously, as if he's been waiting all day just for that moment. There's an undeniable bond between us, one that has only strengthened over the six wonderful years we've been partners.

Together, we've journeyed across the UK, making memories that will last a lifetime. Our shared love for football has taken us to some of the most iconic stadiums – from the City of Manchester stadium, where we experienced the roar of the Champions League semi-final between Manchester City and Real Madrid in 2022, to Molineux Stadium in Wolverhampton and the heart-pounding atmosphere of Wolves facing Brentford in 2023. We've even cheered on teams from the English Football League, visiting grounds like those of Tranmere Rovers, Accrington Stanley, Watford, Carlisle United, Sunderland and Preston North End.

It's no exaggeration to say that Sam might just be one of the most well-travelled dogs in the football world! But it's not just about the places we've been; it's about the journey itself. Football isn't just a hobby for me, it's a passion, perhaps my greatest. There's something magical about waking up on a crisp Saturday morning, knowing that an adventure awaits. With Sam by my side, we head out the door, the anticipation of the 3 o'clock kick-off buzzing in the air. Whether it's a Dundee United home game at Tannadice, an away trip to support our team on the road or ticking off a new SPFL ground from our ever-growing list, the experience is richer with him beside me.

Sam isn't just my guide dog; he's my lifeline, my steadfast companion and, above all, my best friend. He has given me more than I could ever have hoped for: the freedom to live life on my own terms. With Sam, I don't just see the world, I experience it in all its vibrant, exhilarating detail. Sam has made it possible for me to pursue my passions, savouring every moment along the way. He's not just a part of my life; he's at its heart.

The impact of the Guide Dogs for the Blind Association extends far beyond the individual partnerships they create. They have fostered a community of support and understanding, bringing together people who face similar challenges and offering them not just a guide dog but a new lease on life. The work they do is invaluable, and their commitment to improving the lives of those with visual impairments is evident in every dog they train, every match they make and every moment of independence that they help to create.

Chapter 4
THE FIRST FIVE – OUR STARTING LINE-UP

The journey to visit all 42 SPFL grounds to watch a live match was about more than just ticking boxes, it was about making history. Sam didn't just become the first guide dog to complete this monumental challenge; he became the first dog *ever* to achieve it, carving out a unique place in Scottish football history.

This achievement was about perseverance, determination and the bond between us. Throughout the journey, Sam was my companion, navigating us through bustling stadiums, train stations and countless unfamiliar places. Together, we experienced the highs and lows of Scottish football, from the roaring celebrations of victory to the quiet moments of reflection after a tough loss. Every step we took, every stadium we entered, Sam was right there by my side, guiding me safely, and sharing in the joy and excitement that football brings.

Before we officially began this adventure, Sam and I had already visited several football grounds. But the clock started ticking only with our first official match on this quest to visit all 42 SPFL grounds. Some of these grounds we visited more than once, revisiting them as part of this dedicated journey. Each return was a new experience, offering fresh perspectives and memories, but the ultimate goal was always the same: completing the 42.

Ground No. 1 Dens Park – Dundee

Ground No. 1 was Dens Park, the historic home of Dundee. Our visit took place on 1 February 2022, and this was no ordinary match, it was the fiercely anticipated Dundee Derby! Under the glow of the evening flood lights, Sam and I found ourselves in the away end – proudly supporting Dundee United, of course.

Derby days are always special, but there's something uniquely intense about the Dundee derby. With the grounds of Dundee and Dundee United literally just 200 yards apart on the same street, this is the closest derby in the UK. No other derby in British football comes close, not even the famous clashes between Everton and Liverpool or Notts County and Nottingham Forest. The rivalry between Dundee's two clubs is steeped in history: they share decades of passionate encounters, often with everything to play for.

The away allocation for this particular fixture was handled by Dundee United, and I was fortunate enough to have the support of Moira Hughes, the club's outstanding Disability Access Officer. She made sure that Sam and I had accessible seating, ensuring Sam had the space he needed to stretch out and be comfortable – a crucial detail on these journeys. Her dedication made the experience smooth and enjoyable, easing any concerns I had about navigating such a high-stakes match.

One of the highlights of this visit was the audio-descriptive commentary, a service that makes football more accessible for fans with visual impairments. The commentator, also named Sam, is a familiar voice to me, as he provides commentary for the home games of both Dundee and Dundee United. It was comforting to hear his voice guiding me through the action, particularly in such a charged atmosphere. Knowing the commentator well added a personal touch to the experience, making me feel more connected to the game despite being in rival territory.

As for the match itself, it wasn't a classic by any means, especially given the intense expectations that come with a derby. The game ended in a goalless draw, a result that probably reflected the cautious approach both teams took that night. But while the match may not have been a thriller, the experience of being at Dens Park for a derby was unforgettable. There's something undeniably special about witnessing a derby at your rival's home ground – the atmosphere, the tension, the sense of history all combine to create a unique experience.

Dens Park itself is a ground rich in history. Dundee, founded in 1893, has a proud tradition in Scottish football. The club has won the Scottish top-flight league title once, in the 1961/62 season, under the management of Bob Shankly, the brother of the legendary Bill Shankly. That same season, Dundee reached the semi-finals of the European Cup, an extraordinary achievement. Though recent years have seen the club bouncing between the top and second tiers of Scottish football, the memories of past glories continue to inspire the team and its supporters.

Our first visit to Dens Park set the tone for the many adventures that lay ahead. It was an evening of camaraderie, football rivalry and a deepening appreciation for the passion that fuels the Scottish game. For Sam and me, it was the perfect starting point on our journey to all 42 SPFL grounds, a journey that would ultimately lead us to places we had only ever dreamed of visiting.

Ground No. 2 McDiarmid Park – St Johnstone

Only a few days after our visit to Dens Park, on 5 February 2022, Sam and I found ourselves heading to another beloved football ground: McDiarmid Park. This time, our journey was to see Dundee United take on St Johnstone in the SPFL Premiership. McDiarmid Park holds a special place in my heart for several reasons, making each visit feel like a homecoming of sorts.

My connection with McDiarmid Park goes beyond being a football fan. I had the privilege of working there for a year, an experience that allowed me to witness first-hand what a truly well-run community club St Johnstone is. The club's ethos is cantered on inclusivity, and the staff are some of the most dedicated and passionate people I've ever had the pleasure of working alongside. They don't just work for the club, they embody its spirit, pouring their hearts into making sure that everyone, whether player, fan or visitor, feels welcomed and valued.

St Johnstone is renowned for its efforts to make football accessible to all, and this is largely thanks to the incredible work of Bev Mayer, the club's Supporters Liaison Officer and Disability Access Officer. Bev is a force of nature; her dedication to her role is nothing short of inspirational. She's respected not only within the SPFL but also at clubs across the UK for her unwavering commitment to ensuring that all supporters, both home and away, have the best and most inclusive experience possible. Her passion for accessibility in football has set a high standard, and her work has undoubtedly made the game more enjoyable for countless fans, myself included.

In preparation for our visit, I reached out to Bev to let her know that Sam and I would be attending the game. True to form, she went above and beyond, organising seats in an accessible area where Sam would have plenty of space to relax. She also arranged for the audio commentary headset, a service that St Johnstone has been offering since 1990 through the local hospital radio team. It's worth noting that St. Johnstone is one of the longest-running providers of this service in Scotland, a testament to their commitment to accessibility and inclusivity.

McDiarmid Park itself is a relatively modern stadium, built in 1989, and was the first purpose-built all-seater stadium in the UK. Named after local businessman Bruce McDiarmid, who donated the land on which the stadium was built, it has since become a key venue in Scottish football.

As for the match itself, it was another lacklustre affair, both teams failing to find the back of the net. The goalless draw was a result that did little to excite the fans. But for me, the match was about more than just the scoreline. It was about the experience, the atmosphere and the sense of belonging that I always feel when I visit McDiarmid Park.

Every time I return to McDiarmid Park, I experience the warmth and hospitality that the club extends to all its visitors. There's something special about the way St Johnstone goes out of its way to ensure that everyone can enjoy the beautiful game. It's a feeling of inclusion and respect that resonates deeply with me, and it's why I always look forward to our visits.

In the context of our quest to visit all 42 SPFL grounds, McDiarmid Park stands out not just for the matches played on its pitch but for the connections made and the memories created off it. It's a place where football's true spirit shines through.

Ground No. 3 Firhill Stadium – Partick Thistle

We made our trip to Firhill Stadium, the home of Partick Thistle Football Club, on 12 February 2022, and the air was thick with the kind of excitement that only a Scottish Cup 5th round match can bring. On this day, Partick Thistle was facing Dundee United, so Sam and I found ourselves in the away section, ready to cheer on our team.

In the week leading up to the game, I reached out to the club to discuss the accommodations I would need. The club's response was warm and welcoming, which immediately put me at ease. They arranged for audio-descriptive commentary for the match, and made sure that there was accessible seating available in the away end for both Sam and me, ensuring that we were comfortable and well looked after during our visit. This level of care and attention to detail left a lasting impression on me and spoke volumes about the club's commitment to inclusivity and accessibility.

Firhill Stadium, affectionately known simply as Firhill, has been the home of Partick Thistle since 1909. Situated in the Maryhill area of Glasgow, the stadium is more than just a football ground, it's a cornerstone of the local community. Firhill has seen its fair share of footballing drama over the years, from the highs of promotions to the lows of relegations, and everything in between. The stadium has a capacity of just over 10,000, giving it an intimate atmosphere that makes every match feel special. There's a sense of history here, of battles fought and victories won, that you can almost feel as you walk through the turnstiles.

On this particular day, however, the pitch at Firhill was anything but pristine. I remember vividly how the commentator described the conditions – the grass was heavily worn, with patches of mud scattered across the field. It had rained heavily in the days leading up to the match, and the ground had struggled to cope with the deluge. By the time Dundee United's mostly white away strips took to the field, it didn't take long for them to become caked in mud. The commentator's voice painted a picture that made it easy to visualise the players battling not just their opponents but also the elements.

The game itself was a tense affair, as Scottish Cup ties often are. There was a palpable sense of urgency in the air, both teams knowing that a place in the next round was at stake. The first half was closely contested, with chances for both sides, but it was Dundee United who broke the deadlock. In the 34th minute, Ian Harkes found the back of the net, sending the away fans, myself included, into raptures. It was a well-taken goal, the kind that makes all the difference in a cup tie. As the game wore on, the conditions on the pitch became even more challenging, but Dundee United held firm, and when the final whistle blew, it was their name in the hat for the next round.

The experience at Firhill that day was memorable for many reasons. The victory, of course, was sweet, but what stayed with me even more was the sense of community and camaraderie that filled the stadium. We may have been in the away section, surrounded by fellow Dundee United supporters, but it was clear there was a mutual respect between the fans. Partick Thistle is a club that prides itself on being a welcoming place for all, and that was evident in the way they treated Sam and me. A pair of Partick Thistle supporters even walked us back to the subway station to ensure that we got back to Glasgow Queen Street railway station and the train home.

Firhill Stadium itself is steeped in history. Originally built as a multi-sport venue, it hosted not only football but also rugby and even greyhound racing at one point. The main stand, known as the Colin Weir Stand, is named after one of the club's most famous supporters, who was instrumental in saving the club from financial ruin. This stand, along with the rest of the stadium, provides a close-up view of the action, making you feel like you're part of the game rather than just a spectator.

In the years since our visit, I've often reflected on how important these football pilgrimages are to me. Each stadium we visit tells its own story, and Firhill is no different. It's a place where the love of the game is palpable, where history is made with every kick of the ball. And for Sam and me, it's another chapter in our own story – a reminder of the places we've been, the challenges we've overcome, and the joy that football brings into our lives.

Partick Thistle, with its rich history and welcoming spirit, is a club that embodies the very best of Scottish football. And Firhill, with its character and charm, is the perfect home for such a club. As we left the stadium that day, muddy but elated, I couldn't help but feel grateful for the experience. It's memories like these that made our journey across Scotland's football grounds so special.

Ground No. 4 Pittodrie Stadium – Aberdeen

Pittodrie Stadium – one of the coldest football grounds in all of the UK? It certainly feels that way. Nestled right on the north-eastern coast of Scotland, the stadium is regularly exposed to the biting winds that sweep in off the North Sea. On 26 February 2022, Sam and I felt the full force of that icy wind as we stood in the away end, bracing ourselves against the chill to watch Dundee United take on Aberdeen in the SPFL Premiership.

Despite the cold, there was something special about this match, something that went beyond the game itself. The day before, Aberdeen had unveiled a statue of their legendary former manager, Sir Alex Ferguson, right outside the stadium. Sir Alex, who led Aberdeen to unprecedented success in the 1980s, including winning the European Cup Winners' Cup in 1983, was in attendance for the game. Seeing his statue, a tribute to one of football's greatest managers, and knowing he was there, lent the occasion an extra layer of significance.

Aberdeen, known as The Dons, was founded in 1903. Pittodrie, their home ground, is one of the oldest football stadiums in Scotland, having been their home since 1903 as well. Originally, the stadium had a capacity of over 60,000, but today it holds just over 20,000 fans.

Before the match, I was in contact with Lynn Fiske, the club's Supporter Liaison Officer and Disability Access Officer. Lynn was incredibly helpful, ensuring that Sam and I had seats in the accessible seating area and arranging for audio-descriptive commentary. When we arrived at the stadium, Lynn personally came over to greet us and make sure we were settled in, a gesture that made us feel truly welcomed.

As the game kicked off, the wind howled through the stands, a constant reminder of Pittodrie's exposed location. Despite the conditions, the match was a hard-fought affair, Dundee United and Aberdeen battling it out on the pitch. When the final whistle blew, the scoreline stood at 1-1, a fair result for a game where both teams gave their all.

As the crowd began to disperse and the cold seemed to bite even harder, Sam and I made our way back to Aberdeen train station, reflecting on the day. We haven't been back to Pittodrie since that chilly afternoon, but the experience left a lasting impression. The warmth and hospitality of the Aberdeen staff contrasted sharply with the coldness of the weather. It's memories like these that make the journey to each football ground so special, and I'm certain that Sam and I will return soon!

Ground No. 5 New Central Park – Kelty Hearts

Kelty Hearts is one of the newer members of the SPFL, having climbed up from the Lowland League. They quickly made a name for themselves, demonstrating that their ambitions were just as fierce as those of the more established clubs in the league.

Our visit to their ground, New Central Park, on 23 April 2022, was no ordinary match day. It was a celebration, a day that would go down in Kelty Hearts' history. It was the final day of the 2021/22 season, and the anticipation in the air was electric. Kelty Hearts had secured the League Two title in their debut season in the SPFL, and this was the day they would be presented with the League Two trophy in front of their home fans.

From the moment we arrived at the ground, the warmth

and community spirit of Kelty Hearts were palpable. The day was hectic, but they still made time for us. Sam and I were welcomed with open arms, and accessible seating allowed Sam the space he needed to stretch out.

New Central Park, though not the largest stadium, has a character all its own. It's a ground steeped in the local community, where every supporter feels like part of the club's extended family. The passion of the fans, many of whom have followed Kelty Hearts through their rise from the junior leagues to the professional ranks, was on full display. The ground was packed, with a large crowd gathered to witness the culmination of a remarkable season.

The match itself was a hard-fought affair against Forfar Athletic, and although it ended in a 1-1 draw, the result was almost secondary to what was about to unfold. As the final whistle blew, the excitement in the stands reached a fever pitch. Fans pressed against the barriers, eager to catch a glimpse of the trophy that represented so much more than just a title; it symbolised the journey taken by Kelty Hearts, the hard work, the determination and the unwavering support of their community.

It was then that a member of the club's staff approached us and invited Sam and me to come through the barrier onto the pitchside. I was taken aback by their kindness, especially on such a momentous day. As we stood there, just feet away from the players who had given everything for their club, I felt an overwhelming sense of community spirt. Sam, as always, was calm and composed, but I couldn't help but feel that he too sensed the importance of the moment.

When the trophy was finally lifted, the roar from the crowd was deafening. It was a moment of pure joy, of shared pride – and we were right there in the middle of it all. Kelty

Hearts, a club that had risen from humble beginnings, was now a champion, and we were honoured to be part of that historic day.

As we left New Central Park, I couldn't help but reflect on the club's journey, a journey not unlike our own, full of challenges, victories and the unwavering support of a community. We left feeling not just welcomed but truly connected to the spirit of the club. It's a day I'll never forget, and a testament to the fact that in football, it's the people, the community, that make it all worthwhile.

Chapter 5
INTO DOUBLE DIGITS

Ground No. 6 Ibrox – Rangers

Sam and I have had the pleasure of visiting Ibrox Stadium twice, each occasion leaving us with fond memories and a deep appreciation for the hospitality we received. Our first visit was on the very chilly afternoon of 18 December 2021, and the second was on 8 May 2022. Both times, we found ourselves in the away end, cheering for Dundee United as they faced off against Rangers in the Scottish Premiership. The logistics of attending a match can be daunting for the visually impaired, but the experience was made seamless, thanks to the brilliant efforts of John Speirs, the Disability Access Officer.

John's dedication to ensuring that all supporters, home or away, have an enjoyable experience at Ibrox is commendable. In the week leading up to each game, he personally reached out to us, ensuring that Sam and I had accessible seating and organising the arrangements for audio-descriptive commentary. It's worth noting that Rangers are part of the 60% of clubs in the top two divisions of the SPFL providing this essential service, allowing us to follow every pass, tackle and goal with the same intensity as any other fan in the stadium.

Rangers is one of the two towering giants of Scottish football alongside their fierce city rivals, Celtic. Founded in 1872, the team has become synonymous with success, having secured a record 55 Scottish League titles. However, the club's journey has not been without its challenges. In 2012, Rangers faced a financial crisis that rocked the football community, leading to administration and, ultimately, liquidation. It was a dark chapter, but Rangers' resilience shone through as they climbed back from the lower divisions to reclaim their place at the summit of Scottish football, culminating in their 55th title in 2021, a moment of immense pride for their supporters.

John Speirs was a constant throughout both of our visits, doing all he could to ensure our comfort. Not only did he check in on us during the game, but he also made sure we safely navigated our way out of the stadium and down to the Glasgow Subway station. His care and attention ensured that Sam and I could catch the subway back to Glasgow Queen Street station, to board our train home.

Reflecting on these experiences, I'm reminded of how football has the power to bring people together, to create memories that transcend the final score. For me, it's about more than just watching a match, it's about the journey, the camaraderie, and the small acts of kindness that make it all possible. It's not unusual to see the same familiar faces in the away end at Dundee United away games, and I love the friendships that are created. No matter if we win, lose or draw, these friendships make every away trip worth it, and with Sam by my side, I'm able to continue living my passion, unburdened by the limitations of my visual impairment. Together, we navigate the world of football, one match at a time, with each game at Ibrox serving as a reminder of the enduring spirit of the sport and the people who make it special.

Ground No. 7 Victoria Park – Ross County

Ross County is one of the most northern professional football clubs in the United Kingdom, and often mistaken as the furthest north, though that title belongs to Elgin City. The day Sam and I travelled north to visit Ross County is etched vividly in my memory. It was the final day of the 2021/22 season, 14 May, and the anticipation was palpable. Our beloved Dundee United had just secured a fourth-place finish in the league, guaranteeing us a spot in the Europa Conference League play-offs for the following season. The excitement was almost tangible, and over 2,000 Dundee United supporters made the trek north to Dingwall, turning this away day into one of the most unforgettable experiences of my life.

Ross County, known as The Staggies, have a fascinating history. Founded in 1929, the club has spent much of its existence in the lower tiers of Scottish football. However, their story took a significant turn in 2012, when they were promoted to the Scottish Premiership for the first time. This marked the beginning of a new era for the club, and they have since established themselves as a respected team in the top flight. One of their greatest achievements came in 2016 when they won the Scottish League Cup, defeating Hibernian in a thrilling final. It was a historic moment for the club and the community of Dingwall, a small town that lives and breathes football.

Our journey to the Highlands that day was filled with a sense of adventure and a dash of the unreal. As we arrived in Dingwall, the town was buzzing with excitement. The United supporters had turned the place into a carnival, with inflatable beach balls bouncing through the air, and the chant of 'We're all going on a European tour, a European tour, a European tour!' echoing through the streets. The atmosphere was electric, a celebration of a season that had exceeded our expectations.

In the week leading up to the game, I had phoned the Ross County ticket office to inquire about accessible seating in the away end and to let them know that I would be accompanied by my guide dog, Sam. The club's response was nothing short of exemplary. They assured me that the stewards would be informed and that they would be on the lookout for us to help locate our seats.

I was also looking forward to meeting up with a good friend of mine, Gavin Neate. Gavin was in Inverness, so we arranged to meet there and then travelled together by train to Dingwall. The journey itself was beautiful, with the Highland scenery providing a stunning backdrop as we chatted about life and football.

The match itself was everything we could have hoped for. Dundee United emerged victorious with a 2-1 win over Ross County, and as the final whistle blew, the United fans erupted in joy. A massive pitch invasion ensued, with fans streaming onto the field, celebrating not just the win but the culmination of an incredible season. The party atmosphere was infectious, and as I stood there, soaking in the scene, I couldn't help but feel a deep sense of pride and happiness. It was one of those rare moments where everything seemed to align perfectly – the result, the atmosphere and the shared experience with thousands of fellow supporters.

Ross County's Global Energy Stadium, also known as Victoria Park, may be one of the smaller grounds in the Premiership, but it stands at the heart of Dingwall, and the stadium is a place where the passion for football is palpable, and the community's support for their team is unwavering. Despite the size of the town, Ross County has consistently punched above its weight, competing against much larger clubs and often coming out on top.

As Sam and I made our way back to the train station, I couldn't help but reflect on the day. Football has a unique way of bringing people together, creating bonds that transcend the game itself. That day in Dingwall was a perfect example.

Ground No. 8 Easter Road – Hibernian

Easter Road, the historic home of Hibernian Football Club, has stood proudly in Edinburgh since 1893. It's a place full of family tradition, where generations of Hibs supporters have gathered to cheer on their team through thick and thin. Sam and I first visited this iconic ground on 14 January 2023, drawn by the prospect of another away day to watch our beloved Dundee United take on Hibs in the SPFL Premiership.

From the moment we arrived, it was clear that Hibernian was more than just a football club; it was a community, a family that welcomed everyone with open arms. There's something special about Easter Road, a certain warmth that seems to permeate the very walls of the stadium.

Hibernian has a rich history, not only in Scottish football but also in the community. The club prides itself on being inclusive and welcoming, and Joyce Harvie, the Disability Access Officer, exemplifies these values. On our most recent visit, she ensured that we had everything we needed. Her dedication to making Easter Road a welcoming place for all supporters is commendable.

Our visits to Easter Road have included some special moments, like the Europa Conference League play-off against Aston Villa on 23 August 2023. It was a night that saw Scotland star John McGinn return to Easter Road, the very ground where he once wore the green and white of Hibernian. The atmosphere was electric, with Hibs fans turning out in force to see their team take on one of the English Premier League's giants. That night, Hibs were defeated 5-0, but the occasion still demonstrated the club's spirit and the passion of its supporters.

Joyce ensured we had a great experience during the matches, and then invited Sam and me to be part of something even more meaningful: a consultation event with visually impaired Hibs supporters as a guest speaker. I was given the opportunity to speak about my experiences using the audio-descriptive commentary service at Easter Road, as well as at other football grounds across the UK. It was an honour to share my story with some visually impaired Hibs fans and also the two brilliant commentators, George and Alastair, who often provide commentary on match days for visually impaired supporters. Their dedication to making the game accessible to everyone is inspiring, and it was a privilege to be part of such an important discussion.

Every visit to Easter Road reinforces the feeling that Hibernian is more than just a club, it's a family. The care and attention given to ensuring that every supporter feels welcome is what sets Hibs apart. It's a place where Sam and

I have always felt at home, and I look forward to each visit, knowing that we'll be greeted with warmth and kindness.

As we leave Easter Road after each match, I always carry with me a sense of gratitude – for the football, yes, but more importantly, for the people who make the experience so special. Hibernian is a club with heart, and that's what makes it one of the most beloved and well supported in Scottish football.

Ground No. 9 Gayfield – Arbroath

I have to admit, I have a deep affection for Arbroath. Though my heart bleeds Tangerine as a passionate Dundee United supporter, I reserve a special place for Arbroath. There's something charming about this club, something that pulls me in every time I visit. The journey to Arbroath itself is always a delight, a short, scenic train ride along the east coast, where the rolling waves of the North Sea keep you company as you approach the quaint, picturesque harbour town of Arbroath. There's a warmth in the air – not from the weather, which is often anything but warm, but from the people. The townsfolk are always welcoming, greeting visitors with genuine smiles and kind words. The walk from the train station to Gayfield Park winds through the narrow streets and down to the coast, making for a simple pleasure, and I never tire of it.

Yet, there's one thing that always hits you the moment you approach Gayfield. The cold! Situated right on the edge of the North Sea, Gayfield Park is notorious for its bone-chilling winds. On a blustery day, the wind can cut like a knife, and it's no wonder Gayfield is often dubbed one of the coldest football grounds in the UK. But even that doesn't deter me; in fact, it adds to the character of the place. The cold is just part of the experience, a reminder that you're somewhere special, somewhere that's seen decades of football history unfold.

Sam and I have made the trip to Arbroath several times now, each visit memorable in its own right. Our most recent journey to Gayfield was on 4 August 2023, for the opening day of the SPFL Championship season. It was a day charged with anticipation and emotion. Dundee United, after a dismal season that saw us relegated from the SPFL Premiership, were looking to start our comeback with a bang. And what a start it was! We dominated the match, cruising to a 4-0 victory, setting the tone for what would be a triumphant season. That win felt like the beginning of a new chapter, a step back towards where we belong, and as the season unfolded, we did indeed go on to win the SPFL Championship and secure our promotion back to the Premiership for the 2024/25 season.

No matter the result, there's always a deep respect for Arbroath and what they represent. Gayfield is one of those classic, old-school football grounds, full of character and history. Three sides of the ground are still terraced, allowing you to experience the game in a way that feels increasingly rare in modern football. The main stand, with its seating, offers a slightly more sheltered view, but the essence of Gayfield lies in those terraces, where the heart and soul of the club's support gather, braving the elements for their beloved team. Despite the challenges that such an old ground can present, Arbroath have made sure to provide accessible seating areas in the main stand, ensuring that everyone can enjoy the game.

One of the things that further deepened my fondness

for Arbroath was the club's decision to partner with The Guide Dogs for the Blind Association during the 2023/24 season. Arbroath threw their full support behind the charity, organising various fundraising events and raising awareness in creative ways. Guide dog puppies still in training were chosen to walk out with the players onto the pitch as mascots – a season highlight. The sight of those little heroes-in-training stole the hearts of many, and the clip quickly went viral on social media, even catching the attention of well-known figures like Lorraine Kelly and Gary Lineker. The club also took the extra step of releasing a special third kit, featuring the Guide Dogs' blue and yellow colours, complete with the charity's logo on the socks, a symbol of the club's commitment.

For Sam and me, visiting Gayfield has become something of a tradition. Each trip to Arbroath is more than just a football match; it's a chance to reconnect with a community that feels like home, even if it's not our own. There's a real sense of belonging at Arbroath, a feeling that you're part of something bigger, something that matters. The supporters, the staff, everyone involved with the club exudes a warmth that's rare in football, and it's a big part of why I look forward to each visit.

Arbroath may be a small club in a small town, but they're big on heart, and that's what makes every trip to Gayfield Park so special. I always leave with a smile, no matter the scoreline, because the experience of being there, surrounded by such genuine passion and community spirit, is what football is all about.

Ground No. 10 Somerset Park – Ayr United

Somerset Park, home of Ayr United, is one of those iconic old-school football grounds that carries a sense of nostalgia the moment you step foot inside. There's something undeniably special about these traditional venues, where the echoes of past matches seem to linger in the air, and Somerset Park is no exception. It's a place where you can almost feel the history and passion of Ayr United's loyal supporters, a club that has been a cornerstone of Scottish football since its formation in 1910.

Sam and I have had the pleasure of visiting Somerset Park only once, but it's a visit that has stayed with us. It was an away day with Dundee United during the 2023/24 SPFL Championship season, on 26 August. We took the train down to Ayr, which is a journey I've always enjoyed. There's something about watching the Scottish countryside roll by, with its rugged beauty, that's incredibly calming. The train ride gave us time to reflect on the upcoming match, filled with the usual mix of excitement and nerves that come with being an away supporter!

Somerset Park is conveniently close to the train station, just a short walk away, but this proximity meant we didn't get much of a chance to explore much of Ayr itself, an oversight I hope to rectify on a future visit. Ayr is a town steeped in history, known as the birthplace of Robert Burns and for its beach that has been attracting tourists since the arrival of the railway in the 19th century.

At the time of our visit, construction was still ongoing at Somerset Park. Ayr United had embarked on an ambitious project to modernise the ground, building a new stand featuring a state-of-the-art hospitality lounge and other facilities designed to boost the club's revenue. It's clear that Ayr United is a club that's looking to the future while still respecting its rich heritage. The new stand has since opened for the 2024/25 season, and I've heard nothing but glowing reviews. I'm eager to return, not just to see the new facilities, but to soak in the atmosphere that only a ground like this can provide.

On our visit, we were, of course, in the away end. Somerset Park's away section is all terracing, which added to that wonderful old-school feel. There's something raw and authentic about standing on the terraces, surrounded by fellow supporters, sharing in the collective hope and tension that only football can bring. You feel every kick, every tackle and every moment of drama that unfolds on the pitch.

The match itself was one to remember for all the right reasons. Dundee United put in a dominant performance, and we left Somerset Park with a resounding 3-0 victory under our belts. As the final whistle blew, Sam and I couldn't help but grin from ear to ear. There's nothing quite like the joy of an away win, especially in a place as atmospheric as Somerset Park. The walk back to the train station was jubilant, filled with the kind of post-match analysis and chatter that comes after a good result. We boarded the train with big smiles and three points safely in the bag, feeling that familiar warmth of satisfaction that comes with a job well done.

But beyond the result, what really struck me about Somerset Park was its sense of community. Ayr United might not be one of the biggest clubs in Scotland, but it's a club with a big heart. The supporters are passionate, the staff are dedicated, and there's a love for the game that permeates the whole place. It's a club that embodies the spirit of Scottish football – gritty, resilient, and deeply connected to its roots.

I can't wait to return to Somerset Park, to experience it all over again, and to see how the new developments have enhanced what was already a fantastic footballing venue. Until then, the memories of that day, of the songs from terraces, the cold wind biting at our cheeks, and the sweet taste of victory, will keep Somerset Park firmly in my heart.

Top 5 Pies of the 42

A half-time pie is a tradition at football matches.
Here is our Top 5 from our journey around the 42:

1. Kilmarnock – The Killie pie is a must try for any football fan!

2. Bonnyrigg Rose – The Buffalo Chicken pie

3. St Johnstone – The pies at McDiarmid Park are all excellent

4. Greenock Morton – The kebab pie

5. Forfar Athletic – The Forfar bridie! Not a pie, but a must try when visiting Forfar.

Chapter 6
2020

For a couple of years, I fell out of love with football, a statement that would have seemed unimaginable to me at any other time in my life. The year 2020, and the 18 months or so that followed, was a time of unprecedented challenge, fear and loss for everyone, largely due to the global pandemic. The virus swept across the world, forcing us into lockdowns, isolating us from loved ones and upending the normality we all took for granted. Life as we knew it ground to a halt, and with it, my passion for the beautiful game waned, buried beneath the weight of grief and uncertainty.

At the start of 2020, I was in a place of cautious optimism. Sam, my guide dog, had been with me for a little over a year. We were just beginning to hit our stride as a team after a rough period of adjustment following the early retirement of Zorba. That had been a devastating blow; Zorba had seen me through some of the most challenging moments of my life. The bond between a person and their guide dog is one of deep trust and mutual reliance, and to lose that so suddenly had shaken me.

But with Sam, I was slowly rebuilding. He was a typical Labrador, full of energy and love, and he had a natural ability to bring a smile to my face, even on the darkest days. By the start of 2020, we were in a good place, confident, connected and ready to take on the world together. And then, the world stopped.

When the lockdowns began, it felt unreal, almost like living in the pages of a dystopian novel. Like everyone else, Sam and I were allowed out for only one bit of exercise a day, whether it was for a walk, a run or a trip to the shops for essentials. The streets were eerily quiet, the usual hustle and bustle of daily life replaced by an almost oppressive silence. It was strange, unsettling and deeply isolating. On our daily walks, the usual interactions with neighbours or passers-by were gone, replaced by cautious glances and the mandatory two-metre social distancing. The world felt smaller and colder, and I found myself retreating inward, losing touch with the things that once brought me joy.

The year 2020 would soon prove to be the worst year of my life. It began in January with the loss of my granny, a woman who had been a constant source of love and support. She had been in the hospital since December, and I remember the early morning phone call from my auntie – actually my granny's sister – telling me that it was time. Sam and I took a taxi to the hospital, where I met my auntie and my younger brother. We sat by my granny's side, and soon afterwards she slipped away peacefully in her sleep. The grief was immediate and overwhelming. I had been quite close to my granny; she was someone I visited often, someone who always had a smile and a kind word for me and who had made sure to have a treat for Sam. Her loss left a void in my life that I struggled to fill.

Then, in February 2020, just as I was beginning to process my granny's passing, my mum was taken into the hospital. She had been ill for years, suffering from severe arthritis that left her in constant pain. Over the years, she had undergone multiple surgeries – two knee replacements and a hip replacement – but the relief was always temporary, and the pain would return, often worse than before. In 2019, she had one of her knee replacements redone because the joint wasn't moving properly, causing her significant discomfort. By the time she was admitted to the hospital in February, she was in quite rough shape, but there was a flicker of hope. During my visits with her, I noticed she seemed more upbeat, more like her old self. It was a small but significant improvement, and for a brief moment I allowed myself to believe that she might actually get better.

But then the news started to filter in from Europe: the virus was spreading, and it was only a matter of time before it reached Scotland. When the first cases were confirmed, the hospitals imposed strict visitor restrictions, and I could see the impact it had on my mum. Her spirits were dampened. And then, on 23 March 2020, the UK government announced a national lockdown.

My younger sister had been living in New Zealand, but flew back to Scotland in February when mum was admitted to hospital. And now, like the rest of us, she was stuck. New Zealand had closed its borders, and the UK was in lockdown. We were trapped in a limbo of waiting, hoping and fearing the worst. Mum's health started to deteriorate rapidly, and to make matters worse, she contracted Covid while in the hospital. When we were allowed to visit her, it was under strict conditions with masks and aprons.

On 14 May 2020, my mum passed away. She was just 53 years old. The grief hit me like a freight train. All the emotions I had buried after my dad's death in 2010 came flooding back. Losing my mum during the pandemic was especially cruel. The strict social distancing rules meant that even her funeral was a muted affair: no large gatherings, no proper church service, just a small group of close family members gathered at the graveside as the minister spoke about Mum and her life and all the things she loved, and read a passage. It was a heartbreaking farewell.

By the summer of 2020, as restrictions began to ease slightly, I felt numb. I was still living in Newburgh at the time, and though I was now able to travel short distances and meet with friends, I felt like I was going through the motions. My friend Gavin visited, and we walked through the local park with Sam. It was a small comfort, a brief respite from the overwhelming sense of loss and confusion that clouded my days. I also began visiting my auntie again, sitting outside in her garden, chatting while Sam chased a tennis ball. These moments were a lifeline, but they couldn't shake the pervasive sense of emptiness that had taken root in my heart.

During this time, football, the sport that had always been my passion and escape, felt distant and unimportant. The leagues had resumed, but with strict limitations: no fans, empty stadiums and matches played in silence save for the commentary. It was as if the soul of the game had been stripped away. Watching football on television without the roar of the crowd, the chants, the atmosphere, felt hollow. The magic was gone. For the first time in my life, I found myself not caring about the results, not feeling the thrill of a last-minute goal or even the sting of a loss. Football had become a shadow of itself, and in turn, I felt like a shadow of myself.

This period taught me something I hadn't fully realised before: it's the fans who make football what it is. The passion, the noise, the sense of community, that's what gives the game its heart. Played without it, football was just a game played on a pitch, stripped of its emotional depth and connection. It wasn't just the sport I missed; it was everything that came with it – the camaraderie with fellow supporters, the rituals of match day, the feeling of being part of a club.

In August 2020 I also moved to Perth. This was much more convenient, being closer to a main railway station and easier for us to travel. It is also a bit closer to family too.

Returning to football grounds when the restrictions were finally lifted was nothing short of cathartic. It was more than just going to a match; it was a reconnection with a part of myself that had been lost during those dark months. Standing in the stands, surrounded by the noise, the energy, the life of the crowd – it was like waking up from a long, numbing sleep. It reminded me that, even in the hardest of times, the things we love can bring us back to ourselves.

Chapter 7
THE HEART OF THE JOURNEY

Ground No. 11 Caledonian Stadium –
Inverness Caledonian Thistle

Our journey to the Caledonian Stadium in Inverness has been one of profound highs and poignant lows, each visit etched with memories that will stay with me and Sam forever. The first time we made our way to this iconic Highland ground was on 23 September 2023. We found ourselves in the away section, our hearts pounding with excitement and anticipation as we travelled north to support Dundee United in their SPFL Championship clash against Inverness Caledonian Thistle. The thrill of an away day, coupled with the scenic train journey up to the Highlands, made this trip one I had been looking forward to.

Our second visit, however, carried a different kind of weight. On 18 May 2024, we returned to Caledonian Stadium for the second leg of the Championship play-off, a match that would ultimately mark a low point for Inverness Caley Thistle. It was the game that saw them relegated from the Championship to League One, a heartbreaking moment for the club and its loyal supporters as Hamilton

Accies secured promotion to the Championship at their expense. The atmosphere that day was heavy with the gravity of the occasion, a stark contrast to the buoyant spirits of our first visit.

Inverness Caledonian Thistle, as many know, was born from the merger of Caledonian and Inverness Thistle in the 1990s. The idea was to create a unified team that could represent the Highlands on the national stage, competing for trophies and bringing pride to the region. Despite their relatively short history, the club has achieved some notable successes. Perhaps their most famous moment came when they won the Scottish Cup, defeating Celtic in a match that was a testament to the unpredictability and magic of Scottish football – and which produced the legendary newspaper headline 'Super Caley Go Ballistic Celtic Are Atrocious'.

Both times Sam and I visited Caledonian Stadium, we were treated with incredible kindness and professionalism by the club staff. On our first visit, we were greeted by David Scott, the club's Disability Access Officer and Safety Officer. Going out of his way to ensure that Sam and I were comfortable, he showed us to our seats in the away end and made sure there was an accessible space where Sam could stretch out. This attention to detail and genuine care made all the difference, turning what could have been a challenging experience into a truly enjoyable one.

Our second visit was particularly special, as it marked the beginning of our foray into the world of football media. By this time, our journey to visit all 42 SPFL grounds had started with Hamilton. This meant we had access to the press box, both before and after the game, and the opportunity to interview the managers of both teams. It was a thrilling experience, one that I'll never forget because it marked my first steps into football content creation and reporting, something I've grown increasingly passionate about.

After the game, I had the chance to conduct a one-on-one interview with Hamilton's manager, John Rankin. He's a former Dundee United player, which made the moment even more significant for me. I'd be lying if I said I wasn't nervous – this was my first interview with a manager, after all – but John was fantastic. He was gracious and patient, and his team's promotion to the Championship only made the conversation flow that much easier. I'll always be grateful to him for those few minutes of his time that day.

Back in the press box, we had the opportunity to interview Inverness Caley Thistle's manager, Duncan Ferguson. Known affectionately as Big Dunc, he's a man with a formidable presence, both on and off the pitch. Having just suffered relegation, he wasn't in the best of moods. This was the first time the club had dropped to League One in their history. Even so, he took the time to speak with us. I remember asking him about James Carragher, the son of Jamie Carragher, who was on loan at Inverness from Wigan Athletic at the time. When I inquired if another loan spell might be on the cards for the young defender next season, Big Dunc's response was as direct as they come: a flat-out no, due to the number of artificial pitches in League One. James isn't too fond of them, apparently. It was a candid admission, one that gave me a glimpse into the no-nonsense approach that has defined Duncan Ferguson's career.

Despite the ups and downs of the matches themselves, what stood out the most from our visits to the Caledonian Stadium was the warmth and professionalism of the staff. They ensured that Sam and I had the most accessible and enjoyable experience possible, and I'll always be thankful.

Travelling to all the SPFL grounds via public transport comes with its own set of challenges. Anyone who regularly uses trains in the UK knows exactly what I mean. Navigating train stations as a visually impaired person can be daunting, but an app called Passenger Assist has been a game-changer. It allows you to book assistance in advance, ensuring that a member of the station staff meets you when you arrive, helps you to your train, and finds you an accessible seat. It's a service that works flawlessly – most of the time.

The evening after the play-off, Sam and I had booked a taxi to take us back to Inverness railway station, where we were due to catch a train home. I had arranged assistance for a train leaving around 9.30 p.m., and we arrived at the station with plenty of time to spare, around 8.55 p.m. But as we entered the station, I noticed something odd. The place was deserted, with hardly anyone around except for a couple of staff members. I sat down, scrolling through my phone, but after 10 minutes, the station was still eerily quiet. My train was due to leave in about 20 minutes, so I walked up to the gate and told the staff member on duty that I had assistance booked for the train heading back to Perth.

To my disbelief, he informed me that there wasn't another train leaving the station that night; the last one had departed about 45 minutes ago. I was stunned. I showed him my booking confirmation on the Passenger Assist app on my phone, and he radioed his manager to check. After some investigating, it turned out that the system had let me book assistance for a train that doesn't actually exist!

And the next train back to Perth wasn't until 9 a.m. the following day.

The station manager, realising the mistake, contacted Control to see what could be done. He returned with an offer: they would cover the cost of a hotel for the night, and we could catch the train back in the morning. While I appreciated the offer, it wasn't practical; I didn't have anything with me for Sam, including dog food! After some back and forth, Control was adamant about the hotel being the only option.

Just as I was about to resign myself to this, a stroke of luck appeared in the form of a man who had been sitting outside in a private hire replacement bus for the past four hours. He was there to transport passengers from Inverness railway station to Kirkcaldy but had been completely overlooked by the station staff. As soon as the station manager realised this, he asked if the driver could drop us off in Perth on his way back. After getting the green light from Control, we were finally on our way home.

It was a day filled with unexpected challenges, but in the end, everything worked out, and we made it back to Perth safely. Despite the hiccups, our visits to the Caledonian Stadium remain some of the most memorable in our journey across Scotland, not just because of the football but because of the kindness and humanity we encountered along the way.

Ground Nos. 12 and 13 New Douglas Park – Clyde and Hamilton Academical

The journey to New Douglas Park was one that Sam and I had been looking forward to for some time. On 19 January

2024, we made our way to Hamilton for a Scottish Cup tie that promised to be a fascinating game. The match saw Clyde, a side in SPFL League Two, face off against SPFL Premiership team Aberdeen, a daunting challenge for any club from a lower league. Yet, what excited me most wasn't just the game itself, but the opportunity to connect with the passionate Clyde supporters and experience first-hand the atmosphere of this shared ground.

Before the game, I met up with a friend who also works at Guide Dogs and is a die-hard Clyde supporter. We arranged to meet in the supporters' lounge at New Douglas Park, and from the moment I stepped inside, I felt a warmth and camaraderie that you don't often find in larger, more commercialised football environments. My friend introduced me to several other Clyde fans, and I was struck by their genuine hospitality. There was an undeniable sense of community among them, a shared bond that went beyond the game itself.

For a club like Clyde, which has endured its fair share of challenges over the years, that community spirit is essential. Since leaving their historic home at Shawfield Stadium in 1986, Clyde has been somewhat of a nomadic club, sharing grounds with several teams over the years. New Douglas Park, the current home of Hamilton Academical, is where they've found themselves sharing for the time being. The ground, with a capacity of around 6,000, is modest but has a certain charm. It's the kind of stadium where you can hear the players shouting on the pitch and where every fan feels close to the action.

The staff at New Douglas Park were nothing short of brilliant. Accessible seating with enough space for Sam to settle comfortably beside me might seem like a small detail, but to me, it means the world. This is the kind of detail that can turn an ordinary match day into an unforgettable experience. As we made our way to our seats, I couldn't help but notice the buzz in the air. Clyde's supporters, though fewer in number compared to Aberdeen's travelling fans, made up for it with their enthusiasm and vocal support for their team.

When the match kicked off, the difference in divisions between the two teams was apparent, yet Clyde's players displayed a level of grit and determination that earned them respect from everyone in attendance. Aberdeen ultimately won the game 2-0, a result that was expected, but Clyde's performance was far from disgraceful. They fought hard, and there were moments in the match when it felt like they might just cause an upset. The pitch, bathed in floodlights, became a stage for these underdogs to show their mettle, and the fans around me applauded every effort.

Despite the loss, I left the stadium that night with a newfound admiration for Clyde. The club, with its rich history and loyal fan base, had left a lasting impression. My affection for Clyde only grew later in the season when Sam and I travelled up to Borough Briggs to watch Elgin City take on Clyde. Once again, it was the Clyde supporters who stood out. They went out of their way to ensure we found our way to the ground and located the accessible entrance. It's moments like these that remind me why I love football so much. It's not just about the game; it's about the people you meet along the way and the connections you make.

Clyde's journey through different stadiums is a testament to their resilience. After leaving Shawfield, a ground they had called home for nearly a century, Clyde moved to Broadwood Stadium in Cumbernauld in 1994. Broadwood was a modern facility, and for a time, it seemed like Clyde had found a new home. However, challenges arose, and the club eventually moved on to share grounds with Partick Thistle at Firhill and now Hamilton Accies at New Douglas Park. Each move has been a new chapter for Clyde, a club with a history of perseverance and adaptation.

New Douglas Park itself is a ground that has seen its share of memorable moments. Opened in 2001, it replaced Hamilton's former home at Douglas Park, which had been demolished in 1995. The new stadium was part of a regeneration project aimed at reviving football in the area, and it has served as a home for Hamilton Academical ever since. Known for its artificial pitch, which can be both a blessing and a curse depending on who you ask, New Douglas Park is a place where the passion of Scottish football is alive and well.

As Sam and I made our way out of the stadium that evening, I couldn't help but feel grateful for the experience. My encounters with the Clyde supporters, both at New Douglas Park and later at Borough Briggs, were reminders of the kindness and camaraderie that exist within the football community. It's these connections that made our journey across Scotland's football grounds so meaningful, and it's why I now have a soft spot for Clyde, a club that, despite its challenges, continues to embody the spirit of Scottish football.

Ground No. 14 Tynecastle Park – Heart of Midlothian

On 23 March 2024, Sam and I embarked on a journey that had become all too familiar, a train ride to Edinburgh, the bustling capital of Scotland. This time, however, our destination wasn't the historic Heart of Midlothian match but a Women's Cup Final between Rangers and Partick Thistle's women's teams.

As we made the short walk from Haymarket Station to Tynecastle, the streets were alive with the voices of supporters from both Rangers and Partick Thistle, who had travelled from Glasgow to cheer on their teams. There was something special in the air, a mix of hope, excitement and the unspoken bond that football fans share, regardless of which team they support. This match was more than just a game; it was history in the making, particularly for Partick Thistle. For the first time in their history, the women's team had reached a Cup Final, and their fans were out in force, determined to savour every moment of this historic occasion.

Tynecastle Park, the home of Heart of Midlothian, better known simply as Hearts, is a stadium rich in history and atmosphere. Situated in the heart of Edinburgh, Tynecastle has been the stage for countless memorable moments since it became the club's home in 1886. The red-bricked facade of the stadium and its towering stands seem to pulse with the history of over a century of footballing drama. This ground is revered by many, not just for its long-standing history, but for the unique closeness of its stands to the pitch, which gives it an intimate feel, almost as if the fans are right there on the field with the players, urging them on with every cheer, every shout, every breath.

In recent years, Tynecastle has undergone significant re-development, modernising the stadium while carefully preserving the old charm that makes it so beloved. The stands have been upgraded, facilities enhanced and new hospitality options introduced, all while keeping the fans at the heart of the experience. For visually impaired supporters like myself, Hearts have made Tynecastle accessible, with spacious accessible seating areas across all four stands and the provision of audio-descriptive commentary that ensures everyone can be part of the match-day magic.

As we settled into our seats, the stadium began to fill with a sea of supporters. The Rangers and Partick Thistle fans had travelled in numbers, and the atmosphere inside Tynecastle was electric, a testament to the growing popularity and importance of women's football in Scotland. The noise was deafening as the teams walked out onto the pitch, and when Partick Thistle scored an early goal, the eruption of joy from their fans was something to behold. It was a moment of pure, unbridled emotion, the kind of moment that reminds you why you fell in love with football in the first place.

Despite the early lead, Rangers showed their class and experience as the match progressed. They took control of the game, and by the final whistle they had secured a 4-1 victory, lifting the cup amid cheers from their loyal supporters. But it wasn't just about the result. The day was a celebration of how far women's football has come, of the dedication and passion that the players and fans bring to the game.

As Sam and I left the stadium, there was a sense of fulfilment, of having been part of something significant. We walked back to Haymarket Station, the afternoon air crisp and filled with the chatter of fans recounting the day's events. Tynecastle had once again shown why it is such a cherished ground, not just for Hearts fans but for everyone who loves football.

As we boarded the train back home, I couldn't help but feel a deep appreciation for the day. And as Sam settled down beside me, content after a day well spent, I knew that this was another memory we would cherish, a day at Tynecastle for a women's Cup Final, and a day of magic.

Ground No. 15 Hampden Park – Queen's Park

Hampden Park is more than just a stadium; it's a place where the heart of Scottish football beats strongest. For many years, Hampden wasn't fully owned by the Scottish Football Association. Instead, it was owned by Queen's Park, a club with a rich history, known for its amateur status and its motto, *Ludere Causa Ludendi* (To Play for the Sake of Playing). For over a century, Queen's Park proudly called Hampden home, sharing its storied history with the national team. But in 2020, a significant shift took place. The SFA purchased Hampden Park from Queen's Park, securing the future of Scotland's national stadium and ensuring that it would remain the beating heart of Scottish football for generations to come.

Hampden Park is a stadium that Sam and I have visited frequently, and each visit has left a lasting impression. Whether it's for the pulsating atmosphere of an Scotland international match or the quiet anticipation before a Cup Final, Hampden always feels special. There's something almost sacred about stepping into the stands, knowing that this ground has witnessed some of the most iconic moments in football history.

One of the most remarkable aspects of Hampden is how it strives to be inclusive. The stadium offers audio-descriptive commentary – the importance of which is impossible to overstate. It lets the blind and partially sighted be part of the experience, feeling every moment of the match as it unfolds. The crackle of anticipation in the crowd, the roar of celebration when the ball hits the back of the net, the palpable tension during those nail-biting moments – all of this is brought to life in vivid detail.

Hampden's significance extends beyond just the matches played on its turf. Opened in 1903, it was once the largest stadium in the world, capable of holding over 150,000 spectators. Its capacity has been reduced to just over 50,000 today, but the sense of significance remains. It's a place where history echoes through every corner, from the stands to the tunnels, and where the memories of footballing greats like Kenny Dalglish, Denis Law and the current generation of Scottish heroes linger in the air.

As Sam and I sit in the stands, I often think about the moments of joy and heartbreak that Hampden has hosted. The thrill of Scotland's qualification for Euro 2020, celebrated here after so many years of waiting, is a memory that still brings a smile to my face. On those nights, Hampden was the embodiment of a nation's hopes and dreams.

But it's not just the big games that make Hampden special. It's the small things too, the familiar noise of the crowd, the sight of fans draped in tartan and waving flags, the feeling of community. Even on quieter days, when Sam and I visit for a lesser-known fixture, that magic is still there. It's a place where football isn't just watched; it's felt in the very bones.

Queen's Park have moved next door to Lesser Hampden now, but it will always be connected to Hampden. Their decision to sell Hampden to the SFA marked the end of an era, but it also paved the way for a new chapter. The club's legacy remains an integral part of Hampden's story, a reminder of the ground's humble beginnings and the enduring spirit of Scottish football.

Chapter 8
BREAKING GROUND

Ground No. 16 Cappielow Park – Greenock Morton

Greenock Morton, a club rich in history and tradition, stands as a pillar of the Inverclyde region on Scotland's West Coast. The town of Greenock, with its rich maritime heritage, lends a unique character to Morton, a club whose loyal supporters are as resilient as the coastal winds that sweep through their home ground, Cappielow Park. For over a century, Cappielow has been the heartbeat of Greenock, a place where generations of fans have gathered to cheer on their beloved team through triumphs and trials alike.

Sam and I embarked on a journey to Greenock on 12 April 2024, to watch Dundee United take on Greenock Morton in an SPFL Championship clash. It was an evening match, and as we travelled towards the west, the skies grew darker, clouds gathering ominously above as if preparing for battle themselves. The anticipation of a night under the floodlights, at one of Scotland's most historic grounds, had my heart racing with excitement.

Steeping into Cappielow Park feels like stepping back in time, where the echoes of past glories and heartaches still linger in the air. The ground, nestled near the River Clyde, is dominated by the towering cranes of Greenock's shipbuilding past, which loom large over the stadium as a reminder of the town's industrial heritage. It's a place that many football groundhoppers consider a must visit, not just for its unique charm but for the sense of history that permeates every corner of the ground.

One of the iconic features of Cappielow is its open terraced areas, where fans are exposed to the elements, rain or shine. This is particularly true for the away section, a terrace lined with old wooden benches that have seen countless seasons pass by. On this particular night, the weather was not on our side. The cold was biting, and the stormy winds swept through the stands with a ferocity that only a West Coast evening can muster. Rain lashed down relentlessly, turning the terraces into a slick, glistening expanse of wet concrete and wood. Yet, there was something undeniably exhilarating about braving the elements, standing shoulder to shoulder with fellow supporters, united in our shared love for the game.

Normally, Greenock Morton offers an audio-descriptive commentary service for visually impaired supporters, but on this visit, the service was unavailable. I was disappointed, but determined to soak in the atmosphere, relying on the sounds of the crowd and the rhythms of the match to guide my experience.

As Sam and I made our way into the stadium, we were greeted by a familiar face, Stan, a dedicated member of the Dundee United staff. Knowing the challenges we might face in the open terrace, Stan arranged for us to be seated in the accessible area just behind the dugouts in the main stand. It was a thoughtful gesture that shielded us from the worst of the storm and allowed us to enjoy the match in relative comfort. We also had an excellent view of the pitch, and I could sense Sam's excitement as the players warmed up, the familiar thud of the ball against the turf filling the air.

One of the standout moments of the evening came just before half-time. A member of Greenock Morton's staff approached the accessible seating area where we were sitting, then took orders for refreshments at our seats, ensuring that those of us with disabilities didn't have to struggle through the busy concourse at half-time. A small act of kindness, but one that made a significant difference in our match-day experience.

As the match kicked off, Dundee United quickly took control of the game, much to the delight of our travelling supporters. The rain pounded the pitch, but our team played with a fire that was undeterred by the conditions. Goal after goal, we edged closer to securing the SPFL Championship title, a testament to the team's determination to bounce back from the previous season's disappointment. The match ended in a resounding 4-0 victory for Dundee United, a result that left Sam and me beaming with pride as we joined the chorus of cheers that echoed through the rain-soaked stands.

Despite the cold, the storm and the lack of commentary, our evening at Cappielow was memorable. There's something special about experiencing football in its rawest form, where the elements challenge you and the history of the ground adds a layer of depth to the occasion. As Sam and I made our way back to the train station, the rain finally beginning to ease, I couldn't help but feel a deep sense of gratitude. We had witnessed a dominant performance from our team in a setting that felt almost mythical, a night under the lights at Cappielow, where the past and present collide in a dance of passion and resilience.

I'm already looking forward to returning to Cappielow Park, hopefully on a calmer evening, to experience the audio-descriptive commentary and to once again feel the pulse of this historic ground. And while the night was cold and stormy, the warmth of the people and the thrill of the game made it an experience I wouldn't trade for anything.

Ground No. 17 Meadowbank Stadium – Edinburgh City

Sam and I made our way to Edinburgh on the evening of 16 April 2024, for another footballing adventure, this time to Meadowbank Stadium, the home of Edinburgh City. There was a sense of anticipation in the air as we boarded the train. This was not just about the match, it was about experiencing a different part of Scottish football, one with its own unique history and character. The match on this evening was a League One fixture between Edinburgh City and Montrose, two teams fighting for points as the season drew closer to its conclusion.

Meadowbank Stadium is located in the heart of Edinburgh, just a stone's throw away from Hibernian's Easter Road, but it has its own distinct feel. It's a modern facility, run by the council, and serves as a multi-sport complex. The first thing that struck me about Meadowbank was its openness. It's the kind of stadium where you can feel the connection between the city and the people. Built for athletics as well as football, the pitch is surrounded by a large running track, which does create a bit of distance between the fans and the action on the field. At first, this worried me: *Will we be able to feel the intensity of the match? Will the atmosphere be subdued by the vast space around us?* But my concerns were quickly squashed by the passion of the Edinburgh City supporters.

Despite being one of the smaller clubs in the SPFL, Edinburgh City has a loyal fanbase that brings energy and enthusiasm to every match. The kids, in particular, stole the show that night, chanting and drumming throughout the game. Their youthful energy was infectious, and an experience that might have been cold and distant instead felt electric. Edinburgh City, despite its size and recent financial struggles, has a deeply committed following, and the fans were determined to make their voices heard.

Before the match, Sam and I were greeted warmly by the club's staff and supporters. There's something special about the smaller clubs in Scotland; they may not have the glitz and glamour of the bigger teams, but they more than make up for it with heart and hospitality. Edinburgh City made us feel welcome from the moment we arrived. The kindness of strangers is something I never take for granted, and on this evening, it was on full display.

Meadowbank Stadium itself, being a council-run facility, was wonderfully accessible. Everything was on one level, making it easy for Sam and me to navigate, and there was ample seating for disabled supporters in the main stand. The modern amenities included accessible toilets, wide walkways and plenty of space for wheelchairs. It's the kind of stadium that caters to everyone, a reflection of Edinburgh's inclusive spirit.

As the game kicked off, the tension on the pitch was palpable. Edinburgh City had been struggling with form recently, and it was clear that both the players and fans were desperate for a win. Montrose, always a tough opponent, came into the game with their own ambitions, and the match quickly became a hard-fought battle of wills. Edinburgh City's supporters, undeterred by the season's difficulties, kept up their vocal support throughout, willing their team forward.

Sam, as always, was by my side, calmly lying beside my seat, his tail occasionally wagging as he picked up on the excitement. The match itself was a tight affair, with few clear-cut chances for either side. But as the second half wore on, the pressure began to mount on Montrose, and the crowd sensed that a breakthrough might be coming. At around the hour mark, that moment arrived. Edinburgh City's player latched onto a loose ball in the box and slammed it home, sending the stadium into raptures.

The noise was deafening as the players celebrated in front of the fans. It wasn't just a goal, it felt like a release of pent-up frustration and anxiety, a moment of collective joy for a club that had been through a tough season. The fans around us erupted in cheers, hugging and high-fiving each other, and for a brief moment all the financial worries and on-field struggles seemed to melt away.

The final whistle blew with the scoreline reading 1-0 in favour of Edinburgh City, and the relief in the air was almost tangible. As we made our way out of the stadium and back towards Waverley Station, I couldn't help but reflect on the resilience of football fans. Whether supporting a top-tier club or a smaller, community-driven team like Edinburgh City, the passion and dedication remain the same.

Edinburgh City, founded in 1928, is a club with a rich history that has seen it rise through the ranks of Scottish football. Though they've never been one of the biggest clubs in the country, their journey from the lower leagues to becoming a solid presence in League One is a testament to the determination of everyone involved. Meadowbank Stadium, while perhaps not the most traditional football ground, has become a home for the club and its fans, a place where memories are made and dreams are chased.

As we boarded the train home that night, I felt a deep sense of satisfaction. Football, in all its forms, has the power to unite people, to lift spirits and to create moments of pure joy. Sam, curled up beside me, seemed content as well, no doubt dreaming of more adventures to come. I left Edinburgh that night feeling grateful, not just for the win but for the reminder that no matter the size of the club or the stature of the stadium, football always finds a way to bring us together.

Ground No. 18 Galabank – Annan Athletic

Sam and I had been looking forward to our journey down to Annan for quite some time. This time, it was to visit Galabank, the home of Annan Athletic, where the SPFL League One fixture between Annan Athletic and Falkirk was set to take place on 27 April. The excitement of exploring a new town in the Scottish Borders made this trip feel even more special.

Annan itself is a small town in Dumfries and Galloway, situated along the Solway Firth, a region full of natural beauty. I had never visited before, and I was eager to see what the town had to offer. Exploring new places is something I treasure deeply, especially since regaining confidence to travel independently with Sam. These football journeys were about much more than the 90 minutes on the pitch, they were about discovery, human connection and pushing the boundaries of what I believed was possible.

As usual, Sam and I took the train down to Annan. It was one of those beautiful spring days that makes travelling around Scotland even more enjoyable. We connected trains in Glasgow, and it was here that we encountered a good number of Falkirk supporters, all travelling south for the game. Falkirk, by this point in the season, had already secured the League title and promotion to the SPFL Championship, so the fans were in fine spirits, looking forward to seeing their team lift the trophy the following week. As we journeyed together, a few Falkirk fans recognised me and Sam from social media, where I had been sharing snippets of our football adventures. We chatted for a while, and it was heart-warming to hear them speak so kindly of our quest.

From Annan station, we made the short, 15-minute walk through the town to Galabank Stadium. This is one of the aspects I love most about these football trips, the chance to explore the towns and cities we visit, especially those I've never been to before. Annan was charming, with its quiet streets and friendly people. There's a unique joy in wandering through a town with a purpose, knowing that at the end of the journey lies a football ground with its own stories, its own atmosphere and its own people.

Galabank is exactly what I had hoped it would be, a small but beautiful football ground, steeped in community spirit and surrounded by the town's picturesque landscape. The ground may not be large, but it exudes a warmth and welcoming vibe that immediately makes you feel part of something special. It's a perfect example of how much football clubs mean to their local communities, and Galabank felt like the beating heart of Annan.

Before the match, the club had reached out to me on social media, having seen that Sam and I were planning to attend. When we arrived, we were met by a friendly staff member who showed us around the ground, including where the accessible seating area was located. It was also a pleasure to meet Ben, who runs Annan Athletic's social media channels and had been in touch with me in the days leading up to the game. It's always lovely when people go out of their way to make you feel welcome.

The club's facilities are excellent, especially considering their size. The clubhouse, which includes a bar and large TV for showing other sports, is fantastic. The accessible facilities are just as impressive, with easy access to toilets and seating, ensuring that disabled supporters enjoy the match comfortably. I couldn't help but admire how well the club was run: it had the feel of a close-knit community, but also the professionalism that comes with a team determined to offer a top experience for its fans.

The match itself was brilliant. Annan Athletic were up against League champions Falkirk, so the odds were stacked against them. Falkirk came into the match full of confidence, and it showed on the pitch as they quickly took control of the game, racing into a 3-1 lead. Despite the deficit, Annan's supporters never stopped singing, urging their team forward, and it was clear that the players were feeding off this energy. I've always admired the resilience of smaller clubs: the ability to keep fighting, even when the odds are against you, is something special.

And fight Annan did. In the last 10 minutes of the game, something magical happened. Annan Athletic mounted a comeback that I'll never forget. It started with a scrappy goal to bring the score to 3-2, and suddenly, the atmosphere in Galabank changed. You could feel the tension, the hope, the belief spreading through the crowd. Then, with just minutes left on the clock, Annan scored again to make it 3-3. The stadium erupted, the joy was palpable, and even though the game had ended in a draw, it felt like a victory for the home side.

For Sam and me, this trip to Annan will always be one of the standout moments of our journey. It wasn't just about the result, it was about the warmth of the people, the beauty of the town and the warm welcome we both received. Galabank, with its modest size and humble charm, had made a huge impression. It's the kind of place that reminds you why football matters so much to so many.

As we made our way back through the town to catch the train home, I couldn't help but reflect on how far I had come. Just a few years ago, the idea of travelling independently to football grounds across Scotland would have seemed impossible. But with Sam by my side, I had rediscovered my confidence, my independence and my love for adventure – all of which had been reinforced by Annan, with its welcoming community and unforgettable match. This was a journey about more than football; it was about personal growth, resilience and the power of human connection. I couldn't wait for the next adventure.

Ground No. 19 Ochilview Park – Stenhousemuir

Ochilview Park, the home of Stenhousemuir Football Club, is a ground that I had been eager to visit for some time. I remember the day vividly, 28 April 2024, just the day after Sam and I had made the long trip down to Annan. This day would be a day of two football matches: one between Stenhousemuir Women and Forfar Farmington, and one completely different but just as special.

Earlier that morning, before heading to Stenhousemuir, Sam and I found ourselves in Stirling at The Peak, an indoor sports centre situated next to Forthbank Stadium, home of Stirling Albion. I was there to meet my friend Gavin, who had invited me along to see Lothian Wolves play power-chair football. Gavin's technology company sponsors the Lothian Wolves, and I had been eager to learn more about this sport and see the players in action.

For those who may not be familiar, powerchair foot-ball is an indoor game designed for people who use electric wheelchairs. These chairs, known as powerchairs, are spe-cially adapted with large metal guards fitted to the front, allowing the players to 'kick' the ball by driving into it at pace. The game is played on a basketball court with teams of four players, including a goalkeeper, and the object is to score goals just like in traditional football. Powerchair football has grown in popularity over the years and is now a vital part of the sporting community. Watching the game, I couldn't help but be moved by the determination and skill of the players. It's a sport that requires tremendous focus and also fosters an incredible sense of teamwork. The athletes were inspiring, reminding me that football, in all its forms, is for everyone.

After the match, Sam and I made the short journey from Stirling to Stenhousemuir for the afternoon game at Ochilview Park which I was excited about finally visiting. Ochilview Park has a lot of charm, and I had heard a fair bit about its unique history and connection to Norway, of all places.

Stenhousemuir Football Club, founded in 1884, may be considered a smaller club in the SPFL, but it is rich in history and community spirit. Their home, Ochilview Park, has been the club's base since 1890, making it one of the more historic grounds in Scottish football. It's a compact ground with a capacity of around 3,700, and like many smaller stadiums, it has a charm and intimacy that larger grounds often lack. What makes Ochilview particularly unique, though, is its unexpected connection to Norway. This relationship began in the early 1990s when a group of Norwegian football fans adopted Stenhousemuir as their Scottish team. Over the years, the bond has grown stronger, and Norwegian supporters now regularly travel to Ochilview for games. The club has even named their main stand The Norway Stand in honour of their Scandinavian fanbase. It's a special connection, one that highlights the power of football to transcend borders and bring people together from all over the world.

We arrived at Ochilview, to a relaxed and welcoming atmosphere. It's one of those grounds where you feel part of the community immediately. Sam and I were greeted warmly by staff and fans alike, and we quickly found seats in the stand, which offered a great view of the pitch. Stenhousemuir may be a small club, but the pride they have in their ground and their history is evident in everything they do.

The game itself was an early afternoon kick-off, and though Stenhousemuir Women lost 2-1 to Forfar Farmington, the match was still thoroughly enjoyable. There's something about watching women's football that feels refreshingly pure; the commitment and passion on display are always inspiring, and it's a reminder that the game is growing in all the right ways. It has been great to see the growth of the women's game over the past few years as well. I always enjoy the family friendly feel to these games.

As Sam and I made our way out of the stadium after the match, I couldn't help but reflect on how much I had enjoyed the day. From watching powerchair football in the morning to experiencing the warmth of the Stenhousemuir fans in the afternoon, the day had been a perfect reminder of the beauty of sport in all its forms. These are the kind of days that make me so grateful for our quest.

I'm already looking forward to returning to Ochilview Park in the future, to feel once again the warmth of the Stenhousemuir community and, of course, to take in another match in this iconic ground that has connections reaching far beyond the borders of Scotland.

Chapter 9
DISABILITY ACCESS IN FOOTBALL

In recent years, European football has made significant strides toward accessibility and inclusion, recognising that disabled fans deserve an equally immersive and engaging experience at matches. Central to this effort is the role of the Disability Access Officer (DAO), a position that is now firmly embedded in the football landscape across Europe, particularly in the UK and, more specifically, in Scotland.

A UEFA Requirement

The introduction of Disability Access Officers became a formal requirement across UEFA member clubs as of the 2017/18 season. This followed Article 35 bis of UEFA's Club Licensing and Financial Fair Play Regulations, which mandates that all clubs participating in UEFA competitions must appoint a DAO. The rule recognises that football clubs have a responsibility, as pillars of their communities, to ensure that their matches are accessible to all fans, regardless of their physical or sensory impairments. By embedding this requirement into the licensing regulations, UEFA has taken a significant step in normalising disability inclusion within football.

While UEFA governs European competition, its influence trickles down to national leagues, and many domestic football associations have adopted similar requirements. In the UK, where football is more than a sport but embedded within our culture, clubs have gradually recognised the importance of accessibility, and the role of the DAO has emerged as a critical bridge between disabled supporters and football institutions. Scottish football, known for its passionate fanbase and community-centric clubs, has embraced this evolution, and many clubs have appointed DAOs to align with UEFA's vision and cater to the needs of their fans.

The Role in Practice

The DAO serves as a vital advocate and point of contact for disabled fans at each football club. Their responsibilities are broad, covering areas that range from practical stadium access to broader issues of equality and respect for disabled supporters.

A key function is to assess and improve the physical accessibility of football grounds. This includes ensuring that wheelchair spaces, ramps, accessible toilets and appropriate signage are all in place and maintained. However, the role goes beyond infrastructure. DAOs also have a duty to create inclusive experiences for fans with sensory impairments, including providing audio-descriptive commentary services for visually impaired supporters, installing hearing loops or offering sensory rooms for fans with autism and other neurodiverse conditions.

In Scotland, where clubs vary significantly in size and resources, the work of a DAO may differ from club to club. At larger clubs like Celtic and Rangers, the role may involve overseeing extensive access programmes, including shuttle services, audio-descriptive commentary and dedicated disability liaison teams. Meanwhile, smaller clubs such as those in the Scottish Championship or League Two might focus more on meeting the basic needs of disabled fans, such as ensuring ticketing arrangements are accessible and that facilities meet the minimum legal standards. Despite these differences, the principle remains the same: a DAO must work to remove barriers, no matter the scale of the challenge.

Collaboration and Advocacy

The DAO doesn't work in isolation. Collaboration is a crucial element of the role, and DAOs often liaise with various stakeholders within the football world. This includes working closely with supporters' groups, local authorities and disability advocacy organisations such as Level Playing Field and AccessibAll. These partnerships allow DAOs to stay informed about best practices and new innovations in accessibility while ensuring that the voices of disabled fans are heard at both the local and national levels.

In Scotland, DAOs often coordinate with clubs' Disabled Supporters Associations (DSAs), which provide direct feedback on the needs and expectations of disabled fans. This two-way communication is crucial to ensure that accessibility measures remain relevant and are continually improved. By listening to the fans themselves, DAOs can tailor their efforts to meet specific local needs, whether it's improving access routes in rural stadiums or providing better services for disabled fans travelling to away games.

Challenges and Progress

While the introduction of the DAO is a positive step, the journey towards full accessibility is ongoing. Scottish football grounds, many of which are steeped in history, present particular challenges. Older stadiums like Firhill, Hampden Park and Tannadice were built long before accessibility standards were prioritised, meaning that retrofitting them with modern access features can be both technically difficult and expensive. This has created a disparity across the league, and some clubs are able to offer far more comprehensive services than others. However, the presence of a DAO at every club ensures that accessibility remains a priority, even when resources are limited.

Moreover, the role of the DAO extends beyond infrastructure and physical access. In many cases, DAOs must address the cultural and attitudinal barriers that can exist in football, helping to educate staff, stewards and other fans about the importance of accessibility and respect for disabled supporters. They must foster an inclusive atmosphere where disabled fans are welcomed and feel comfortable attending matches, knowing that their needs will be met.

A New Era for Scottish Football

In Scotland, where football's cultural significance is immense, the role of the DAO represents a shift toward a more inclusive future. Clubs have begun to recognise that accessibility isn't merely a legal or regulatory obligation but a moral one, reflecting the very spirit of the game. Football is, and should always be, for everyone.

By ensuring that disabled fans are accommodated, respected and valued, the DAO helps to create a footballing environment that celebrates diversity. And in a country where community is at the heart of every football club, this is a responsibility that is deeply felt. The efforts of DAOs are helping to make the terraces and stands of Scottish football more open and welcoming than ever before.

In many ways, the role of the DAO is just the beginning of a broader transformation. As attitudes toward accessibility continue to evolve, and as clubs become more attuned to the needs of all supporters, Scottish football is poised to lead by example – not only in Europe (the audio-descriptive commentary is now offered as a service to supporters at 71% of Scotland's top two divisions - the Premiership and Championship) but on the global stage. In doing so, the sport will become what it has always strived to be: a place where everyone can belong.

Disabled Supporters Associations

Disabled Supporters Associations (DSAs) play an essential role in ensuring that football is accessible to everyone. In the UK, and particularly in Scotland, DSAs act as the crucial link between disabled fans and football clubs, advocating for better facilities, policies and an inclusive match-day experience.

Football has always been about bringing people together, and yet, for a long time, many disabled supporters were left out of the experience due to inadequate access and

A collection of photographs of Jon and his guide dog Sam on their travels

Sam watching the women's Scottish cup final at Tynecastle Park between Rangers and Partick Thistle

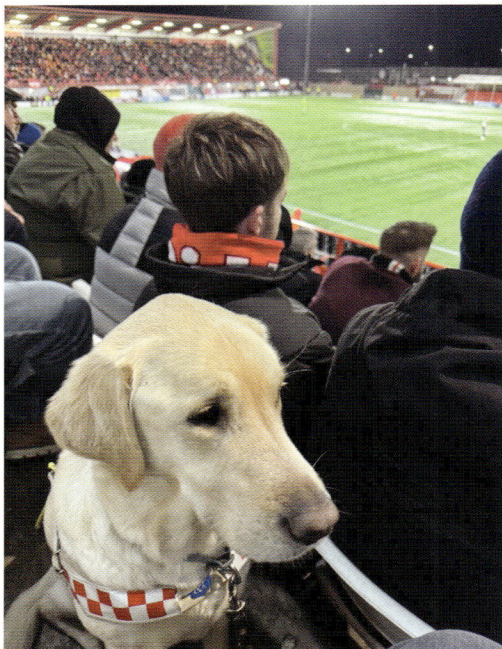

Sam is sitting in the stands at New Douglas Park in the Scottish Cup match between Clyde and Aberdeen

The picture of the Buffalo Chicken pie at New Dundas Park home of Bonnyrigg Rose

Jon with Sam by his side speaking on the panel at the
EFL conference in Walsall in 2023

Jon crouching down beside Sam for a picture while they
were out for a walk at a local park

Jon and Sam in the stands watching a game at
Easter Road stadium

Jon and Sam walking off the Celtic Park pitch following their interview about their journey completing the 42 and just before Celtic played Dundee

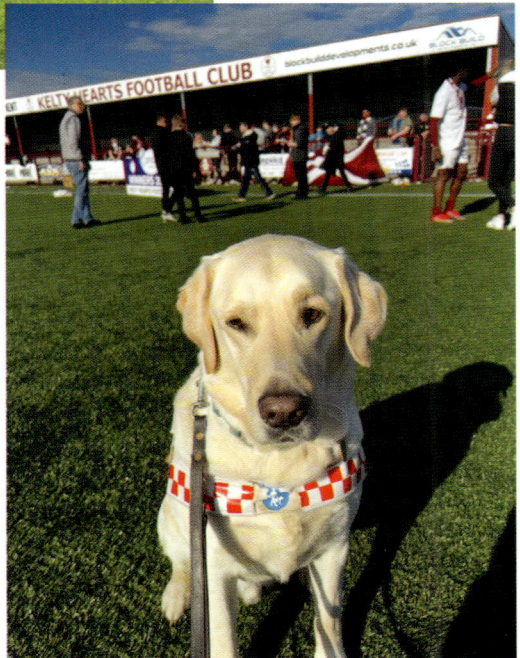

Sam on the pitch at New Central Park, home of Kelty Hearts, after they just won the League Two trophy

Jon and Sam behind the scenes in the Raith TV interview room at Starks Park, home of Raith Rovers

Sam at Borough Briggs, home of Elgin City

Jon and Sam with Celtic manager Brendan Rodgers

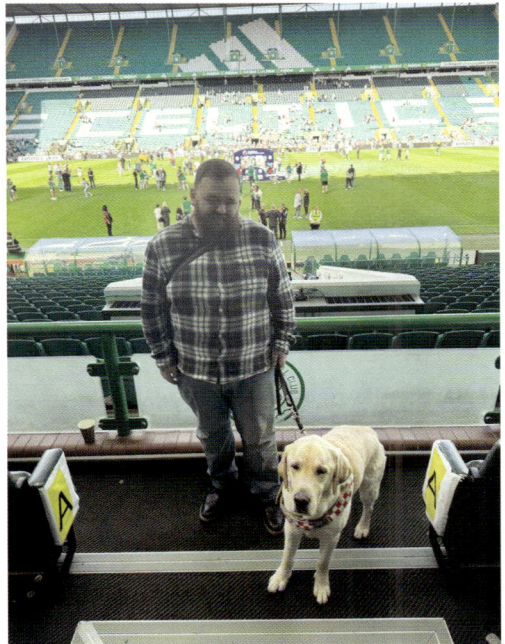

Jon and Sam at Celtic Park after the Celtic women's team had just won the SWPL league title

Jon and Sam at Celtic Park next to the SWPL trophy

Sam lying down in the stands at Airdrieonians

Jon and Sam outside the main entrance to Hampden Park

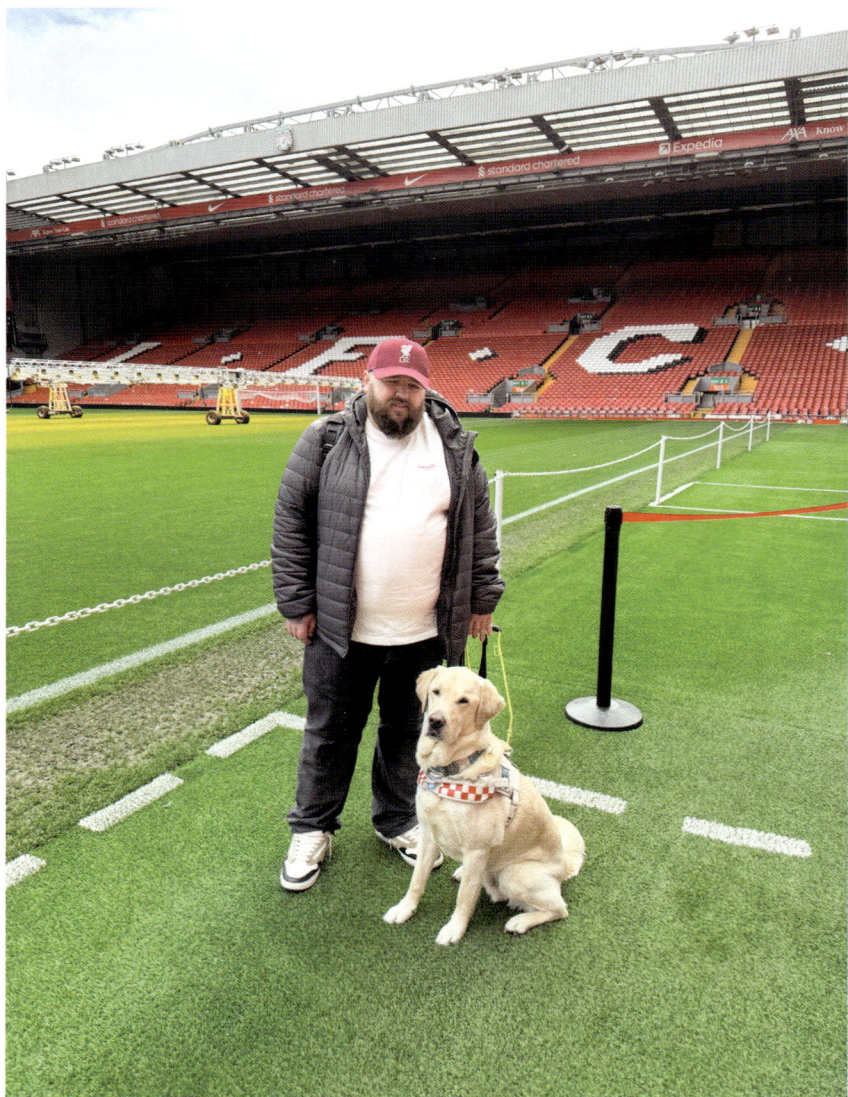

Jon and Sam pitch side at Anfield in Liverpool

Sam meeting another assistance dog at the Champions League
semi final between Manchester City and Real Madrid

Jon and Sam sitting in the stands at McDiarmid Park
home of St. Johnstone

Jon and Sam outside Hampden Park before Scotland v Finland

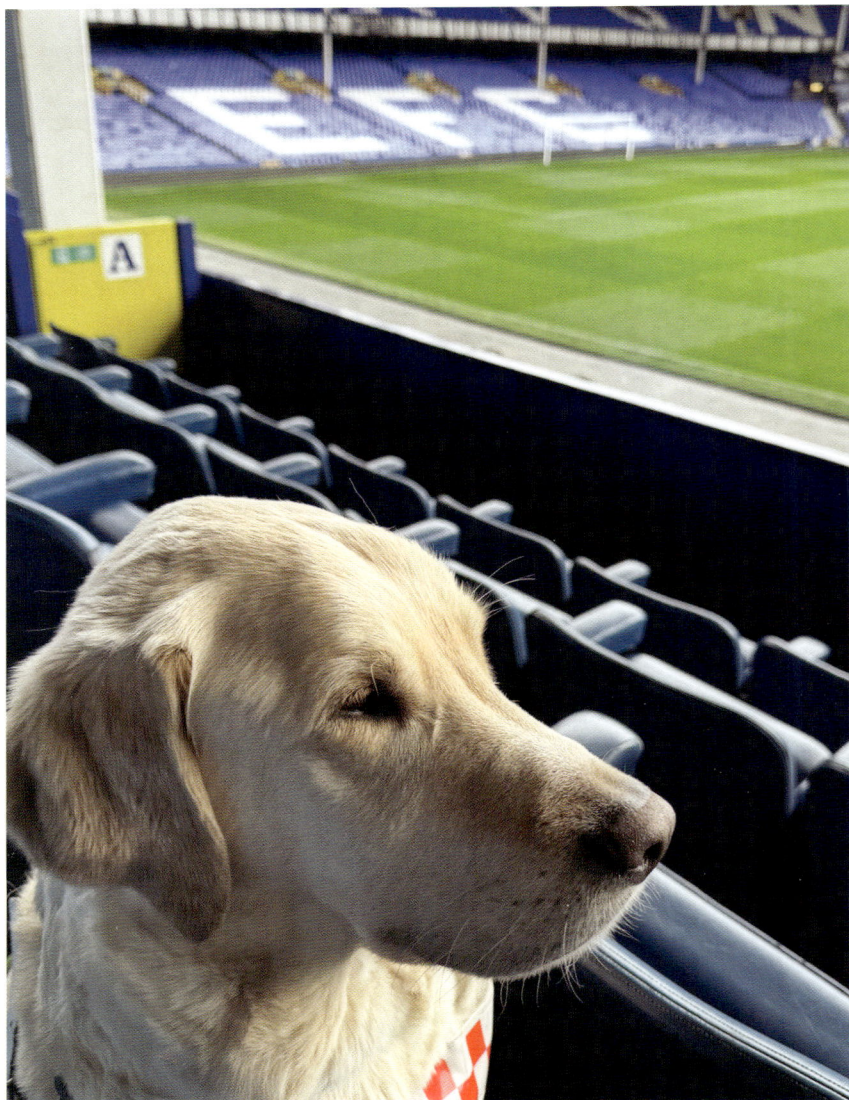

Sam sitting in the stands at Goodison Park,
home of Everton

Jon and Sam on the pitch at Station Park, home of
Forfar Athletic, after being presented with an award
and medal by the SPFL for completing the 42.
Photo credit: Christopher Coutts (SPFL)

Jon and Sam at Hampden Park after completing the 42
with Sam wearing his SPFL medal

seating arrangements, or simply a lack of understanding from clubs. DSAs emerged as a vital resource to bridge this gap, representing the needs and concerns of disabled fans directly to football clubs. In Scotland, this has become a significant movement, with a lot of clubs in the SPFL now having established their own DSAs.

These associations serve as both advocates and a community for disabled supporters. They offer a platform for fans to voice concerns and, more importantly, to work collaboratively with the club to find solutions. Whether it's ensuring wheelchair-accessible seating, better sightlines for visually impaired fans or appropriate parking spaces and facilities, DSAs help address these issues. Their work doesn't just stop at infrastructure; they also advocate for accessible ticketing services, steward training and inclusive communication.

A key figure in this relationship is the DAO, who works to ensure that clubs meet the standards required by equality legislation, such as the Equality Act 2010. But the DAO often goes beyond legal obligations to create a welcoming and supportive environment for disabled fans. In Scotland, the DAO is often the first point of contact for disabled supporters, whether they're regular attendees or visiting fans.

One of the most influential organisations supporting DSAs and DAOs across the UK is Level Playing Field. This charity promotes accessibility and inclusion in football, offering resources, advice and advocacy for disabled supporters. It works closely with football clubs, DSAs and DAOs to improve stadium access, provide training and raise awareness of the importance of inclusivity in sports. Level Playing Field has been instrumental in encouraging football clubs to take proactive steps towards inclusivity, pushing for accessible facilities and more opportunities for disabled fans to engage with the sport.

In addition to Level Playing Field, AccessibAll (formerly known as CAFE, the Centre for Access to Football in Europe) plays a pivotal role on a broader, international scale. AccessibAll's mission is to ensure that football is accessible to everyone, everywhere, regardless of disability. They work with clubs, national associations and governing bodies across Europe to improve accessibility in football. In Scotland, their influence can be seen in how clubs like Celtic, Rangers and Hearts have worked to modernise their stadiums and services to meet the needs of disabled supporters.

AccessibAll also provides resources for disabled fans travelling to international matches, ensuring that supporters have the information they need to access stadiums, facilities and transport when following their teams abroad. Their guidance, combined with the support of DSAs and DAOs, has been crucial in making football a more inclusive space for fans with disabilities.

The progress that has been made in Scottish football is significant, but there is still work to be done. The Scottish FA, SPFL and individual clubs must continue to listen to DSAs and DAOs to ensure that all supporters, regardless of ability, feel included in the match-day experience. DSAs, along with Level Playing Field and AccessibAll, have been at the forefront of this fight, ensuring that football is a game for everyone. Through their advocacy, the experience for disabled fans in Scotland has improved dramatically, and they will continue to play a vital role in shaping the future of accessibility in football.

For me, as a disabled supporter myself, it's inspiring to see the work these organisations and individuals do to make the game we all love more accessible and welcoming. They have shown me that football truly is for everyone, and as I've experienced on my journey around Scotland's football grounds, the efforts of both DSAs and DAOs can make all the difference in ensuring every fan can enjoy the sport.

Chapter 10
START OF THE SECOND HALF

By this point in the journey, Sam and I had begun to build a following on social media as people became more invested in our mission to visit all 42 SPFL grounds. What started as a personal adventure for me and Sam was quickly turning into something much bigger, resonating with football fans and supporters far beyond the stands.

At each ground we visited, I began to record short videos of our travels, little glimpses into what the experience was like from our perspective, and I shared them on X and TikTok. Initially, I did this to document the journey, but as I kept posting, I realised it was also an opportunity to raise awareness about something that was deeply important to me: accessibility in football. I wanted to shine a light on the fantastic work that many SPFL clubs were doing to make their grounds more accessible and to create a welcoming atmosphere, and I felt that this was something that didn't always get the recognition it deserved.

More than anything, I hoped that by sharing our journey, I could encourage other disabled supporters to attend a game at their local club, perhaps for the first time. The idea of going to a football match can be daunting, especially if you're unsure about what you might encounter, particularly in terms of accessibility. I wanted to change that. I wanted people to see that, yes, it's possible to have an incredible day at the football, no matter what your circumstances.

And the response was heart-warming. I received messages from people who had never been to a game before but were now considering it. It was humbling to know that Sam and I were making an impact, that our journey was inspiring others to take that first step towards enjoying live football.

One thing I really felt passionate about promoting is the availability of services like audio-descriptive commentary – football's best-kept secret in my view. The commentators are specially trained to describe the game in vivid detail. It's a game-changer, quite literally, but is not always well publicised. Yet, for many visually impaired supporters, it will be the difference between deciding to go to a game or staying home. I knew that the work so many people at these clubs were doing to make football accessible deserved more attention, and I wanted our journey to give their efforts the spotlight.

Each time we posted a new video or shared another update, it wasn't just about Sam and me ticking off another ground, it was about showcasing how football can include everyone. It was about creating a ripple effect, one that I hoped would lead to more and more disabled fans feeling confident enough to come and experience the beautiful game in person, just as it should be.

Ground No. 20 Albert Bartlett Stadium – Airdrieonians

The Albert Bartlett Stadium has seen several name changes over the years, a common trend for football grounds.

However, when Sam and I made our visit on 1 May 2024, it was still widely recognised by its earlier name, the Excelsior Stadium. This trip wasn't for an Airdrieonians game but for a highly anticipated derby in women's football, as Celtic Women's team took on Glasgow City. There was a buzz in the air, and you could feel the intensity that comes with any Glasgow derby.

Celtic Women's team currently play most of their home matches at this ground, though they also occasionally grace Celtic Park. Sam and I have had the pleasure of attending their matches at both venues, each with its own distinct charm. This match at Excelsior Stadium, however, held a special significance. Once again, Celtic provided the much-appreciated audio-descriptive commentary service which makes all the difference for me, enabling me to follow the action on the pitch. Celtic have been trailblazers in this area: they were the first club in Scotland to offer this service at their women's matches, and for that, I'll always be grateful.

The journey to Airdrie was straightforward enough, starting with a train to Glasgow Queen Street station before changing for the final leg to Airdrie. It was our first time visiting the town, and after a pleasant 20-minute walk from the train station, we arrived at the stadium. There's something exciting about visiting a ground for the first time; it's a fresh chapter in the journey, and Airdrie certainly didn't disappoint.

The stadium is relatively modern compared to some of the older grounds Sam and I have visited. It was completed in 1998 and has a capacity of just over 10,000. Despite its modest size, it's well maintained and offers a great view of the pitch from almost any seat. The club that calls it home was founded in 1878 as Airdrieonians and enjoyed some glory years, most notably winning the Scottish Cup in 1924 and reaching the Cup Final again in 1992. This century, in 2002, the club was reformed as Airdrie United.

On this occasion, the focus was firmly on the women's game. Celtic and Glasgow City have been dominant forces in women's football in Scotland, and this showed on the pitch. The game was fiery and competitive, and though it ended in a 2-2 draw, this scoreline was a fair reflection of the match. There were moments of brilliance from both teams, but no side could quite find the edge to take all three points.

As we made our way back to the station after the match, I couldn't help but feel grateful for the journey we were on. Each ground we visit, each match we experience, adds another layer to the story, and this night in Airdrie was one I won't forget.

Ground No. 21 Borough Briggs – Elgin City

To reach Elgin, the most northern home of professional football in the UK, Sam and I embarked on what felt like a long journey! After a scenic train ride to Inverness, we transferred onto another train that took us deeper into the Highlands, to Elgin, where Elgin City was set to host Clyde at Borough Briggs.

I had never been to Elgin before, and as we stepped off the train into this picturesque town, I was struck by its beauty. Borough Briggs, a stadium with an old-world charm, is just a short 15-minute walk from the station, and I found myself appreciating the quaint streets and the gentle buzz of activity. The sun cast a golden glow over the buildings, and there was a music festival nearby, filling the air with distant tunes that floated through the streets.

But as much as I was enjoying the surroundings, exhaustion had caught up with me. Sam and I had been travelling relentlessly over the past few weeks, ticking off ground after ground. The miles had started to weigh, and for the first time on this journey, I felt that I might not make it to the match. As we walked through town, I found a bench near a small lake. The calm waters mirrored the cloudy sky, and the combination of the music, the quiet rustling of the wind and the sheer beauty of the scene was almost enough to convince me to stop for the day. My body was weary, and just for a moment, I considered turning back, heading home and calling it a day. Sam sat by my feet, patiently waiting as he always does, but even he seemed to sense the weight of my fatigue.

I let the thought linger for a moment, but then the reality hit me: we were here, in Elgin, just minutes away from another historic ground on our quest to conquer the 42. If we left now, we'd have to come all the way back. I knew I couldn't quit. Not when we were so close. After taking a few minutes to gather my energy, I stood up and patted Sam. Together, we pressed on towards Borough Briggs.

I must have been more tired than I realised because, as we walked, I completely lost my bearings. The streets all started to blend into one, and I couldn't quite figure out if we were heading in the right direction. I stopped a group of Clyde supporters who were walking nearby and asked if we were on the right path to the stadium. Their faces lit up, and they reassured me we were just minutes away. To my relief, a few of them even walked with us, guiding us to the stadium and helping me find the accessible entrance.

In moments like these, I'm reminded of the kindness that exists in the football community. Despite being rivals on the pitch, fans off it are always willing to lend a hand, and I felt an immense sense of gratitude for their help.

When we finally arrived at Borough Briggs, I was struck by its simplicity and character. Built in 1921, the stadium has an undeniable charm. Like other older grounds, it's mostly terracing, with a small seating area in the main stand. I've always had a soft spot for these types of stadiums. There's something raw and authentic about them, something that connects you to the generations of fans who stood on those same terraces, watching their team play through triumph and heartbreak. Borough Briggs, with its backdrop of the northern sky, felt like a place where time stood still.

The match itself was tense, but ultimately Clyde dominated, securing a 3-0 win. For Clyde, this was a crucial victory that ensured their survival in League Two, sparing them from the relegation play-off. Elgin City, on the other hand, didn't have much to celebrate that day, but the result didn't dampen my experience. There was something about this stadium, the kindness of the fans and the atmosphere of the day that made this one of my favourite grounds to visit on this entire journey. Maybe it was the relief of having made it despite my earlier doubts, or perhaps it was the charm of the town itself, but I left Borough Briggs content.

As Sam and I made our way back to the station, the earlier exhaustion had lifted. The cool evening air revived me, and I found myself reflecting on just how far we had come. This journey, from the bustling cities to the quiet northern towns, had been filled with highs and lows, but every step had been worth it. I boarded the train back to Inverness with a renewed sense of purpose, grateful for the day, for the kindness of strangers and for the unforgettable experience that Elgin had given us.

Ground No. 22 Ainslie Park – Spartans

Sometimes, the best parts of a journey come from the unexpected, the unplanned and the spontaneous decisions that can turn an ordinary day into something unforgettable. That's exactly how I felt on 4 May 2024 as Sam and I made our way back from Elgin. I was tired, yes, but still riding the high of another ground checked off our list. As the train hummed along the tracks, I found myself scrolling through my phone, curious to see what was happening in the world of Scottish football.

That's when I saw it. A match at Ainslie Park, home of Spartans, the very next day. Even better, it was a match between Spartans Women's and my own team, Dundee United Women's. I hadn't originally planned to visit Ainslie Park so soon, but something about the timing just felt right. I didn't think too long; I bought the ticket right there on the train, feeling a surge of excitement. After all, this journey was all about seizing moments and making memories.

Spartans may be relatively new to the SPFL, but they spent many years in the Lowland League before securing promotion. Their home, Ainslie Park, is a modern and intimate stadium located in the north of Edinburgh, with a capacity of around 3,000. It's a ground designed with the community in mind, offering modern facilities and a welcoming atmosphere. Spartans are a club who pride themselves on their community roots, and this ethos was immediately clear when Sam and I arrived.

The morning of 5 May was crisp but sunny, and there

was a relaxed pace to the day as Sam and I boarded the train once again, this time heading to Edinburgh. The stadium itself is tucked away in a residential area, not far from the bustle of the city, yet somehow it feels like its own little football haven.

When we arrived at Ainslie Park, I was struck by how friendly and welcoming everyone was. The staff went out of their way to make sure Sam and I were comfortable. One of the stewards walked with us to the accessible entrance, sharing stories about the club and their pride in how Spartans have grown over the years, both in men's and women's football. There was something incredibly heart-warming about the way the club operated. This wasn't just about the football for them; it was about community, connection and making everyone feel at home.

The game itself was well-attended, with a good number of fans coming out to support their teams on a sunny Sunday afternoon. The atmosphere was lively but relaxed, the kind of place where you feel like you're among friends, even if you're meeting for the first time. Spartans put up a solid fight against Dundee United , and while the match ended in a 0-0 draw, the energy on the pitch never dipped. It was an evenly matched contest, both sides pressing hard, but neither could break through the other's defence.

Even though the match ended without any goals, there was something refreshing about watching women's football at this level, the sense of progress and equality that Spartans clearly championed. I felt proud that Dundee United's women's team was part of a growing movement in Scottish football.

As the match wrapped up and the crowd began to filter out, Sam and I made our way back towards Haymarket station, the sun starting to dip lower in the sky. There was a sense of calm satisfaction as we walked through the streets of Edinburgh, knowing that we had just ticked off another ground on our mission to complete the 42. But this wasn't just another ground. By the time we boarded the train home, I realised that the day had also reminded of why I had set out on this journey in the first place.

For discovery, adventure and the simple joy of following where the game, and Sam, led me.

Ground No. 23 Indodrill Stadium – Alloa Athletic

The season had reached its most dramatic stage: promotion and relegation play-offs. On the evening of 7 May, Sam and I embarked on a short journey to Alloa, brimming with anticipation for the first leg of the semi-final play-off between Alloa Athletic and Hamilton Accies. The stakes couldn't have been higher. The winner of this two-legged affair would move one step closer to a crucial play-off final, where the prize was a coveted spot in the Scottish Championship. The reward? Championship football for the 2024/25 season. The losers, however, would be left to battle it out in League One.

Alloa Athletic's Indodrill Stadium, situated in the shadow of the Ochil Hills, had long been on my list of must-visit grounds. There's something about it – the branding, the history of the club – that makes it feel special, more than just another football ground. Alloa Athletic, known as The Wasps due to their iconic black and gold kit, have a long tradition in Scottish football, dating back to their founding in 1878. Despite being one of the smaller clubs in the SPFL, their sense of community runs deep, and the fans create an atmosphere that makes the Indodrill feel alive on match days.

As we approached the stadium, I could feel the excitement in the air. Though modest in size, with a capacity of just over 3,000, the Indodrill has a character all of its own. Formerly known as Recreation Park, the ground is a mix of old and new, with modern touches like the artificial pitch (one of the few in Scottish football), surrounded by traditional terracing that harks back to a bygone era. It's a place where the passion of lower league football is palpable, and it felt like the perfect setting for a high-stakes play-off.

Sitting there with Sam by my side, as the sun dipped below the horizon and the floodlights bathed the pitch in a glow, I couldn't help but feel a deep connection. The atmosphere was electric, with both sets of fans singing their hearts out, fully aware of what was at stake. The tension on the pitch mirrored that in the stands. Alloa and Hamilton were evenly matched, and you could see it in every tackle, every pass and every shot. There was no room for error.

By the time the referee blew the final whistle, the scoreboard read 2-2, leaving the tie finely balanced. Both teams had shown tremendous spirit, and there was still everything to play for in the second leg. As we made our way out of the stadium, I couldn't help but feel a sense of admiration for Alloa Athletic and their fans. They had shown true heart, fighting toe to toe with a club of Hamilton's stature.

Little did we know at the time, but this thrilling contest was just the prelude to an even more dramatic conclusion. Hamilton Accies would go on to win the second leg, securing their place in the play-off final. There, they triumphed over Inverness Caledonian Thistle across two tense legs, earning their promotion back to the Championship. Meanwhile,

Alloa's season ended in heartbreak, but their performance in the play-offs had shown that, even in the face of tough opposition, they were a club with a fighting spirit, one that will undoubtedly rise again.

Ground No. 24 Forthbank Stadium – Stirling Albion

Forthbank Stadium sits at the heart of Stirling, a city drenched in Scottish history, its ancient castle towering above, and echoes of battles fought long ago still lingering in the air. It's a place where the past meets the present, and on 11 May 2024 Sam and I were set to experience a battle of our own, this one fought not with swords but with boots and footballs as Stirling Albion faced Dumbarton in the second leg of their play-off final.

I'd been looking forward to this visit ever since attending the Women in Football networking event at Hampden Park a few weeks prior. It had been an inspiring day, where I was given the chance to meet some remarkable women who are making waves in the football industry, an industry still very much dominated by men. One speaker, in particular, left a lasting impression: Christine Curtis, Managing Director of Stirling Albion. Her story of resilience, determination and leadership in football, navigating her way through various roles in different clubs, captivated me. Hearing her speak so passionately about the challenges she'd overcome and the triumphs she'd experienced made me even more eager to visit Stirling Albion. This was no longer just about ticking off another ground from the 42; it was about seeing the club that she led with such pride.

The day finally came on that warm May afternoon, with the stakes as high as they get in football. Stirling Albion were fighting for their place in League One after losing the first leg 2-1 at Dumbarton's stadium, known as The Rock. They came into this match needing to overturn the deficit in front of their home fans at Forthbank Stadium. Forthbank, with its striking red and white stands and capacity of just over 3,800, is a relatively modern ground, having been opened in 1993 to replace the club's former home, Annfield Stadium. It sits next to The Peak, a state-of-the-art sports complex, giving the area a vibrant, sporting energy. Though compact, there's something special about Forthbank – thanks to the way the stands are close to the pitch, the atmosphere created by the supporters and the unmistakable feeling of community.

When Sam and I arrived, that sense of community was palpable. From the moment we stepped through the turnstiles, we were greeted warmly by the staff and volunteers, as is often the case at lower-league clubs in Scotland. There's a rawness and honesty about football at this level, no glitz, no glamour, just passion and dedication. The stewards quickly guided us to the accessible seating area at the front of the main stand, ensuring Sam and I were both comfortable.

As the game kicked off, the tension was clear. Sam, usually calm and composed, seemed to sense the excitement. Stirling Albion knew they had to score to keep their League One status alive, but Dumbarton were resolute, defending their slender lead with everything they had. The teams battled back and forth, every challenge hard fought, every pass closely contested. The Stirling fans were in full voice, urging their team on, but the elusive goal never came. As the minutes ticked away, it became apparent that this wasn't going to be Albion's night. Despite their best efforts, they couldn't break down Dumbarton's defence. When the final whistle blew, the scoreboard still read 0-0, and with it came the crushing reality that Stirling Albion would be relegated to League Two for the 2024/25 season.

It was heartbreaking to see the players slump to the ground, dejected, while the fans applauded their efforts despite the outcome. Relegation is a bitter pill to swallow, especially after a season filled with so much hard work. But football, as we all know, can be cruel.

Despite the disappointing result, I couldn't help but feel a sense of admiration for the club. Stirling Albion, affectionately known as The Binos, has a long history. Founded in 1945, they've had their fair share of ups and downs, including stints in Scotland's top tier in the 1950s. Though they've spent much of their recent history in the lower leagues, their supporters remain fiercely loyal, and the club has always been at the heart of the Stirling community.

As Sam and I made our way out of the stadium, I reflected on the afternoon. It wasn't the result I'd wanted for Stirling Albion, but the experience itself was memorable. From the camaraderie of the fans to the hospitality of the club, it was another reminder of why I love Scottish football, especially at this level. The passion, the dedication and the sense of community are what make it so special. The game of football is so much more than just 90 minutes on a pitch.

Chapter 11
THE HOME STRETCH

Ground No. 25 Stark's Park – Raith Rovers

Stark's Park, nestled in the Fife coastal town of Kirkcaldy, has been the proud home of Raith Rovers Football Club since 1891. It's one of the oldest stadiums in Scottish football, and from the moment Sam and I first set foot inside, I felt again a sense of tradition and community. That day, 7 October 2023, was the first of three visits we made to Stark's Park in the 2023/24 season. Our team, Dundee United, were playing Raith Rovers in what would turn out to be a tense and hard-fought Championship match.

As we approached the ground, there was something almost comforting about the sight of the old railway embankment that borders one side of the stadium, a reminder of how connected this club is to the town and its people. Fans were streaming in, many wearing their beloved dark blue and white, with Raith scarves draped proudly around their necks. That game ended in a 1-1 draw, both teams fighting to gain an edge in a league where every point counts. Raith Rovers were having a strong season, and you could sense that they were aiming high, pushing Dundee United to the limit in their pursuit of promotion.

Our second visit was even more dramatic. On 17 May 2024, Sam and I returned to Stark's Park, not just as fans this time, but with media accreditation. Raith Rovers were facing Partick Thistle in the second leg of the Premiership play-off semi-final, and I remember how excited I felt entering the stadium that evening, knowing I'd be watching a match that could change the club's future. Raith had secured a 2-1 victory in the first leg at Firhill, and they were just one match away from the play-off final.

Stark's Park was electric that night, the stands packed with hopeful supporters willing their team to hold onto that narrow advantage. The atmosphere was thick with tension as the game unfolded, both teams giving it their all. I'll never forget the emotion in the crowd as the final whistle blew with the aggregate score tied 3-3, sending the match to penalties. Sam, sensing the anticipation, sat alert at my side. Everyone in the stadium was on edge, and when Raith Rovers finally emerged victorious, winning 4-3 on penalties, the explosion of joy from the stands was incredible. Fans hugged strangers, some in disbelief, others overwhelmed by pride in their team.

For me, that moment also felt personal. To be standing there, witnessing such a pivotal moment in Raith's season, felt like I was part of their story. By this point, I had been sharing videos on X and TikTok for months, and the club had been kind enough to grant us media access for the night. This allowed me to witness the post-match celebrations from a unique vantage point. The sight of the players and staff celebrating with the fans was a reminder of what football can mean to a community.

Just a week later, on 23 May, Sam and I were back again for the Premiership play-off final's first leg, this time against Ross County. The air was thick with anticipation as fans knew that promotion to the top flight was within their grasp. Before the game, Davie Hancock from Raith TV generously gave Sam and me a behind-the-scenes tour of the commentary set-up, offering a glimpse into the work that goes on behind the cameras. It was fascinating to see how much effort and coordination goes into bringing the game to fans who can't be there in person.

The match itself was another nail-biter, with Ross County managing to edge out a 2-1 win. Despite Raith's best efforts, they would ultimately fall short in the second leg up in Dingwall. The disappointment was tangible, but there was also a sense of pride in what the team had achieved throughout the season.

After the final whistle, as the crowds were starting to disperse, I had the incredible opportunity to interview Raith Rovers manager Ian Murray. It was a humbling experience to speak with someone who had led his team through such an intense campaign. Ian's reflection on the game was one of both pride and frustration, acknowledging how far the team had come while also expressing the pain of falling just short. It was the third time I'd interviewed a manager post-match, and I had learned more each time about the intricate emotions that come with being at the helm of a football club.

Stark's Park, with its long history and passionate supporters, has given me memories I'll cherish forever. From the highs of that play-off semi-final win to the more sobering moments after the final, I've come to appreciate not just the football but the resilience of a club and its community, always pushing for that next opportunity.

Ground No. 26 Stair Park – Stranraer

Stair Park, home of Stranraer, is a special place in Scottish football, a small, traditional stadium that has stood the test of time. It's tucked away in the southwestern corner of Scotland, in the coastal town of Stranraer, near the ferry port at Cairnryan that links Scotland with Northern Ireland. On 22 June 2024, Sam and I visited this historic ground for a preseason friendly where Stranraer took on Larne, a team from Northern Ireland's top division.

This was one of the longest trips on our journey to complete the 42, and I had to plan meticulously, knowing that it would be a long and potentially challenging day. Being visually impaired means that every journey requires extra thought, from making sure Sam has everything he needs – water, food and a good rest schedule – to working out train times, connections and contingency plans. The trip to Stranraer was no exception.

The original plan was straightforward: a train to Glasgow, then Glasgow to Ayr, and then a connecting train from Ayr down to Stranraer. However, as is often the case when travelling, things didn't quite go as planned. Upon arriving in Ayr, I learned ongoing rail works meant that the line south of Ayr was closed, and we'd have to take a rail replacement bus the rest of the way to Stranraer – and then back again after the game. This threw a wrench into my carefully constructed itinerary, but I wasn't about to let it spoil the day. I spoke with the ticket office staff at Ayr station, who were incredibly helpful, printing out new schedules and ensuring I'd still be able to get home, though three hours later than expected!

While we were waiting for the bus, a man and his daughter, Derek and Jessica, approached us, having recognised

Sam and me from the posts I'd been sharing on X and TikTok. They were Larne supporters making the trip to Stranraer for the day. They were also Hamilton Accies fans and had visited many Scottish grounds, so we struck up a conversation about our shared passion for football and the journeys it takes us on. That unexpected encounter is one of the things I love most about football. Whether you're travelling alone or with your dog, you're never really alone; there's always a connection waiting to be made with some-one who shares the same love for the game.

Stranraer may not be one of the bigger clubs in Scotland, but it has a proud history. Founded in 1870, the club has long been an integral part of the community, and you can feel that when you step inside Stair Park. The ground itself is a mix of old-school terracing and a more modern main stand – and as we entered the ground, I was struck by how much of its history is on display. Along the back wall of the terraced stand behind the goal, there are photographs and timelines of the club's key moments, a celebration of everything Stranraer has achieved through the decades.

Sam and I made our way to the main stand, where the burger van caught my attention. The smell of sizzling burgers was too tempting to resist, so I grabbed a cheese-burger and chips during half-time while Sam tucked into a bone I had brought along for him. Football is always better with good food, and the atmosphere at Stair Park, with its friendly fans and laid-back vibe, made for a perfect af-ternoon despite the earlier travel hiccups. Sam, ever the sly opportunist, also decided to help himself to some of my leftover chips from my half-time food! I was holding the carton and had bent down to open my backpack, not realising I was now holding the carton with a couple of remaining chips at Sam's eye level. Being a typical Labrador, he took advantage of the opportunity to help himself to the remainder of the chips. Sam's favourite part of any game is, I'm pretty sure, the end when we are leaving and he has the opportunity to sniff around for any leftover pies that might be lying around on the ground!

The match itself was an entertaining affair, especially for an early preseason game. Both Stranraer and Larne looked sharp, and while the final score was 1-1, it didn't feel like a typical low-key friendly. The Larne fans, who had travelled across the water and made the short trip down from the ferry port, brought plenty of energy, and the Stranraer supporters responded in kind. It was a reminder that even in these smaller matches, the passion of football fans remains undimmed.

After the game, we began our long journey back home, once again relying on the rail replacement bus to get us back to Ayr. To my surprise, we ran into Derek and Jessica again, and spent the return journey chatting more about Scottish football, comparing notes on the various grounds we had visited. It's moments like these that make the sometimes frustrating parts of travelling worth it. The camaraderie you find with fellow fans, the shared stories, and the mutual respect for each other's journeys all contribute to the sense of belonging that football creates.

By the time Sam and I arrived home, it had been a 15-hour day, longer than I had anticipated but also one of the most memorable. Visiting Stair Park, experiencing the hospitality of Stranraer, and meeting Derek and Jessica were highlights in themselves. Stranraer may be one of the more remote stops on our tour of the 42, but it left a lasting impression, one that I'll always treasure.

Ground No. 27 Tony Macaroni Arena – Livingston

The Tony Macaroni Arena, nicknamed the Spaghettihad by supporters, stands as one of the more unique venues in Scottish football, but it also proved to be one of the more challenging for Sam and me to reach using public transport. Our journey to Livingston on the evening of 25 June 2024, for a preseason friendly between Livingston and Broxburn Athletic, was a reminder that accessibility in football goes beyond the stadium, and starts with the journey itself.

Livingston, based in West Lothian, has built a reputation as a welcoming and community-oriented club since it was established in 1995, but their home ground poses some logistical challenges for fans like me who rely on public transport. The Tony Macaroni Arena is a modern venue, with an artificial surface and capable of holding nearly 10,000 fans, but its location, on the edge of Livingston's Almondvale area, isn't the most accessible by foot or rail. The nickname Spaghettihad is a nod to the quirky sponsorship – which came to an end in March 2024 – and to the winding roads and roundabouts that surround it, as well as a nod to Manchester City's Etihad Stadium.

I had planned our journey meticulously. We took the train to Livingston North station, and I had arranged to get a taxi from the station to the ground. Livingston itself is a sprawling town, known for its shopping centres and housing estates, but not particularly easy to navigate if you're unfamiliar with the area. For someone who is visually impaired, the prospect of crossing busy roads and roundabouts was daunting, but I had faith in Sam's guiding abilities.

Unfortunately, things didn't go as smoothly as I'd hoped. When the taxi arrived, the driver took one look at Sam and refused to take us, claiming he didn't allow dogs in his car. It's moments like these that remind me of the barriers that still exist for disabled people in society, despite the legal protections we have. Under the Equality Act 2010, it's illegal for taxis to refuse assistance dogs unless the driver has a medical exemption, but sadly, refusals are still all too common. My heart sank as the taxi drove off, leaving us stranded at the station with the clock ticking toward kick-off.

It wasn't the first time I'd been refused service because of Sam, but it never gets any easier. There's always that underlying worry when travelling to new places: *Will we face another refusal? Will I be able to find another way?* After the initial frustration passed, I knew we couldn't give up. I called another local taxi firm, but they couldn't send a car for at least an hour. With less than 45 minutes until the game kicked off, I had no choice but to rely on Sam and my own determination to get us to the ground on foot.

I pulled up Google Maps on my phone, input the directions and set off, trusting Sam to help me navigate the unfamiliar streets. The route wasn't easy – Livingston is notorious for its confusing network of roundabouts and underpasses – but Sam, as always, was confident. In situations like these, I'm endlessly grateful for his calmness. It's not just his ability to lead me safely; it's the way his confidence lifts me when my own is wavering. With Sam by my side, we managed to navigate the streets, crossing busy roads and walking through residential areas until, finally, the Tony Macaroni Arena came into view.

In the days leading up to the match, the club's social media team had been engaging with us after I posted about our visit, and when we arrived at the stadium, I felt an immediate sense of welcome. They displayed a warmth and hospitality that made up for the challenges of getting there. They may be one of the younger teams in Scottish football, but their sense of community and pride is unmistakable. Livingston has a loyal fanbase, and the friendly nature of their supporters shone through during our visit.

The match itself, a local derby against Broxburn Athletic, had a competitive edge despite being a preseason fixture. Broxburn, a small town just a few miles from Livingston, had brought a decent number of travelling fans, and the atmosphere was lively. The game was closely contested, with Livingston narrowly edging out a 2-1 victory. As Sam and I sat in the stands, enjoying the buzz of the crowd, I couldn't help but reflect on how far we'd come that evening – not just physically but mentally as well. Overcoming obstacles, both literal and metaphorical, had become a recurring theme on our journey, and each time, Sam's presence gave me the strength to push through.

After the final whistle, we made our way out of the stadium, where thankfully, the taxi I'd booked earlier arrived without issue to take us back to Livingston North station. We caught the train home, exhausted but content. I left Livingston with fond memories of our visit to the Tony Macaroni Arena, and with hope that our experience might raise awareness of the importance of accessibility, both in football and in society.

Livingston had welcomed us with open arms, and I left with a sense of gratitude toward both the club and their fans. I'm looking forward to the day we can return, hopefully with fewer obstacles along the way.

Ground No. 28 The Rock – Dumbarton

Dumbarton Stadium, often affectionately referred to as The Rock by both fans and football groundhoppers, is one of the most iconic and unique football grounds in Scotland. This name isn't just a clever nickname; it's a nod to the majestic Dumbarton Rock, an ancient volcanic formation that looms over the stadium, with the historic Dumbarton Castle perched at its summit. The sight of the rock face towering over the pitch gives the ground a character and charm that few other stadiums can match. For many football enthusiasts, visiting The Rock is a must-do, and it was certainly a destination that Sam and I were eager to experience.

Dumbarton Football Club, currently playing in SPFL League One, was founded in 1872, the same year as Rangers. It has the distinction of being one of the oldest clubs in Scotland, and has a history rich with achievements, particularly in the early years of Scottish football. They won the first two Scottish League titles in 1891 and 1892. The second title was shared with Rangers after a play-off match ended in a draw, making Dumbarton technically joint champions, a feat that remains a significant part of the club's proud history.

The opportunity to visit The Rock came on 29 June 2024, for a preseason friendly match between Dumbarton and Falkirk. This was one of the grounds I had been most excited to visit, and the day did not disappoint. The anticipation of seeing this legendary ground in person, with its dramatic backdrop and deep-rooted history, made the trip all the more special.

From the moment we arrived, the warmth of the Dumbarton community was palpable. My growing online presence meant that I was contacted by George Drummond, a dedicated volunteer at Dumbarton, who extended an invitation for us to attend the preseason game against Falkirk. George's hospitality was exceptional. He went the extra mile to make our visit memorable, greeting us with a Dumbarton scarf, a club pin badge and a match day programme, thoughtful gifts that I will always cherish. He even treated me to the classic football experience of a half-time pie and a steaming cup of Bovril, a gesture that made me feel truly welcomed.

We were also met by Jacqui Sibbald, the club's Disability Access Officer. Her warm welcome and thorough orientation of the ground were invaluable. She took the time to show us around, making sure we knew where everything was and that we were comfortable in our surroundings. Her dedication to ensuring that disabled supporters have the best possible experience at The Rock was evident, and her friendly presence throughout the day made us feel like we were more than just visitors – we were part of the Dumbarton family.

The match itself, though just a preseason friendly, was filled with the excitement and passion that makes football so special. But it was the overall experience – the people we met, the history we absorbed and the unique charm of The Rock – that made our visit to Dumbarton unforgettable. It's not just the game that sticks with me; it's the sense of community and the feeling that, for that day, Sam and I were woven into the fabric of the club.

Sam and I left Dumbarton that day with full hearts. We'll be returning to The Rock whenever we get the chance. The combination of stunning scenery, a rich footballing heritage and the kindness of the people we met ensures that

Dumbarton will always have a special place in our journey across Scotland's football landscape.

Ground No. 29 Balmoral Stadium – Cove Rangers

Sam and I set off for Aberdeen on 2 July, determined to tick off another stadium on our journey to complete the 42. This time, our destination was Balmoral Stadium, home of Cove Rangers, for a preseason fixture against Dunfermline Athletic. It was one of those typical Scottish summer evenings – dark clouds hung low in the sky, and the rain poured down relentlessly as we made our way to the ground. As the train rattled north, I remember thinking that the weather couldn't have been more fitting for an evening of gritty lower-league football.

Cove Rangers, though relatively new to the Scottish Professional Football League (SPFL), have made their presence felt in a remarkably short period of time. They earned promotion from the Highland League in 2019 and made a meteoric rise through the divisions, reaching the Championship within just a few seasons. Although they faced relegation back to League One, their ambition is clear, and their success story in Scottish football is one that speaks to their determination and strong community backing.

As we arrived in Aberdeen, the rain hadn't let up. Balmoral Stadium, located in the Cove Bay area on the outskirts of the city, felt a world away from the more central venues we'd visited. The stadium itself is modern, having opened only in 2018, and it's clear that the club has big aspirations. With a capacity of around 3,000, it may be small by SPFL standards, but what it lacks in size, it makes up for in character. Despite being one of the newer clubs in the league system, Cove Rangers have cultivated a strong local following, and you could feel that community spirit the moment we arrived.

From the second we stepped through the gates, we were greeted warmly by the club staff. They had been expecting us and ensured that Sam and I were well looked after. One of the stewards came over and guided us to our seats in the stand, making sure we were comfortable and had a good view of the pitch. This can make all the difference for disabled fans, and Cove Rangers went out of their way to make sure we felt welcome. They even pointed out where the accessible toilet was and gave us directions to the main reception area if we needed anything else during our visit. In those moments, the rain didn't matter – it was the warmth of the people that we noticed.

The turnout for the match was impressive, considering it was a midweek preseason fixture and the weather was far from ideal. Dunfermline had brought a decent number of travelling supporters up from Fife, and there was a buzz in the air despite the soggy conditions. Cove Rangers is a small club, but they've got big ambitions, and you could feel the optimism among their fans. They're determined to punch above their weight, a spirit they share with some of the smaller clubs across Scotland and something I've come to admire.

The game itself was not high stakes, but it was still a decent contest. Both teams were getting a feel for the new season ahead, and although preseason matches are often about fitness more than results, you could see the effort on the pitch. Cove Rangers, in particular, held their own against a strong Dunfermline side, and the match ended in a well-earned 1-1 draw. There's something special about watching football in the rain – an added intensity, a sense that every tackle, every pass is just that bit more significant because of the slippery conditions.

As I stood there, rain dripping from my jacket, with Sam faithfully lying at my feet, I couldn't help but reflect on how far we'd come. This was one of the more distant grounds for us to visit, and the weather had certainly added to the challenge. But it's moments like these that make the journey worthwhile. The camaraderie, the welcome from the Cove Rangers community, the resilience of the players on the pitch – it all reminds me why I set out to do this in the first place.

I wanted to experience the heart and soul of Scottish football in all its forms, from the small, community-driven clubs like Cove Rangers to the grand, storied stadiums of the Premiership. Each visit brings its own set of memories, its own unique challenges and joys, and this wet Tuesday night in Aberdeen was no different.

As the final whistle blew, and we made our way back to the train station, I felt a sense of accomplishment. The rain hadn't dampened our spirits – if anything, it added to the story. Cove Rangers had given us yet another fantastic experience, and I knew that this visit would be one of those that stayed with me long after we'd completed the 42. There's something about the smaller clubs, with their die-hard fans and intimate stadiums, that leaves a lasting impression. And Cove Rangers, with their welcoming atmosphere and strong community ethos, had certainly made their mark.

Top 5 Match Atmospheres

The atmosphere at games is often spoken about as something that adds a lot to the experience of match day. These are the Top 5 that Sam and I experienced on our journey around the 42.

1. Dundee Derby – The atmosphere at Dundee derby games is always incredible!

2. Ross County v Dundee United – United had qualified for Europe, it was the final game of the season and there was a carnival-like atmosphere in the away end!

3. Kilmarnock v Cercle Brugge – Sold out on a European night, great experience!

4. Raith Rovers v Partick Thistle – The play-off semi-final finished 3-3 and went to penalties, and the atmosphere was incredible!

5. Celtic Women v Hibernian – The last day of the season, when Celtic won the League title at Celtic Park for the first time

Chapter 12
ADVOCACY

I've always been a passionate advocate for accessibility, not just in football but in all aspects of life. It's been a lifelong commitment to ensure that spaces are open, inclusive and welcoming to everyone, regardless of their circumstances. My journey as a campaigner began long before Sam came into my life, but the importance of this work was made even clearer when Sam became my guide dog and daily companion. The world, which I thought I understood well, became something I had to navigate with an extra layer of vigilance, one where barriers to access are not just inconvenient, but sometimes outright discriminatory.

One of the most frustrating and recurring issues I've campaigned against is access refusal, when guide dog owners and other assistance dog owners are denied entry to businesses and public spaces. This might seem shocking to some, but it's an everyday reality for many people who rely on assistance dogs. Despite clear legislation in place, access refusals remain a persistent issue, not just for me but for thousands of other guide dog and assistance dog owners across the UK.

Under the Equality Act 2010, it is illegal for businesses

or service providers to refuse access to someone with an assistance dog. The law is explicit: guide dogs are not pets, they are working animals, providing essential services to their handlers. This legislation is meant to ensure that we can go about our lives without unnecessary barriers. Yet, despite its clarity, guide dog users still face frequent refusals when trying to enter restaurants, shops, taxis and other public spaces. It's baffling, and frankly infuriating, how often the simple presence of a guide dog is met with ignorance, fear or outright hostility.

I remember one particular incident vividly. On entering a café with Sam, the manager came over immediately, pointing to a sign that read 'No Dogs Allowed' and telling me to leave. I calmly explained that Sam was a guide dog and that, under the Equality Act, he had the right to be there with me. The response?

'I'm sorry, but we don't want dogs in here.'

I left the café, not just upset but disheartened by the reality that this sort of encounter is not an isolated event.

Guide Dogs UK, the charity I've had the privilege of working with on many occasions, reports that over 81% of assistance dog owners have been refused access to a service or business at least once. Think about that for a moment . . . 81%. That's eight out of ten people with guide dogs or assistance dogs being told, essentially, that they don't belong in public spaces, that their needs are secondary to arbitrary policies or prejudices.

Taxis and private hire vehicles are among the worst offenders. Despite it being clearly illegal to refuse someone with a guide dog, there have been countless reports of drivers declining passengers, often claiming allergies, religious beliefs or a simple 'no pets' policy. While some of these reasons may seem acceptable, the law is clear: unless a driver has a medical exemption certificate (which must be issued by the local authority), they must accept guide dogs. And yet, time and again, we hear stories of guide dog owners left stranded at the roadside or forced to make alternative arrangements.

Sam and I have had our fair share of these experiences, from taxis that speed away the moment they see us, to drivers who refuse outright despite my attempts to explain the law. Each time, it leaves me feeling frustrated, not just for myself but for all of us in the guide dog community. We've worked so hard to raise awareness, and yet there is still so much more work to be done.

It's this ongoing struggle that has driven me to campaign for change. In partnership with Guide Dogs UK, we've taken these issues to some of the highest levels of government, both in Scotland and at Westminster. I've attended party conferences for the SNP, Scottish Labour and the Scottish Conservatives, standing alongside other campaigners to bring these issues directly to the attention of those in power. The conversations at these conferences have been encouraging, but there's a long road ahead to turn awareness into action.

One of the most impactful moments in my advocacy work came when Sam and I travelled to Westminster in both 2019 and 2023 to raise these issues with government ministers and MPs. Walking through the historic halls of Parliament with Sam by my side felt like a significant step in our journey. It was a powerful reminder that, even though we were there to speak about discrimination, we had already overcome so much to get to that point. In those meetings, I was able to share my personal experiences and the experiences of others in the guide dog community, and there was a genuine sense that the politicians we spoke to wanted to help. But good intentions aren't enough. We need legislative follow-through, stronger enforcement of the Equality Act 2010 and harsher penalties for businesses that repeatedly break the law.

Beyond the legislative changes, we also need a shift in attitudes. Discrimination against guide dog and assistance dog owners often stems from ignorance: people simply don't know the law, or they don't understand what guide dogs are trained to do. Education, therefore, is key. Campaigns like those run by Guide Dogs UK aim to raise awareness, not just among businesses but among the general public so that people can recognise when an injustice is taking place and feel empowered to speak out.

I've also seen first-hand the positive impact that personal stories can have. When Sam and I share our journey, whether at conferences, in the media or even in casual conversations with strangers, it opens people's eyes to the reality of what life is like with a disability.

Football has given us a unique platform to advocate for change. As we've travelled to stadiums across Scotland, we've seen how clubs can be leaders in accessibility, creating inclusive environments that cater to all fans, regardless of their needs. It's a model that other sectors could learn from.

Through this journey, I've come to realise that advocacy is not just about fighting for yourself; it's about fighting for the next person who walks into that café, or tries to get into that taxi, or walks up to a stadium gate. It's about ensuring that no one else has to face the same barriers we've encountered. It's about making sure the world is a little more accessible for everyone.

As I look back on our campaigns and the countless hours spent advocating for change, I'm proud of what we've accomplished. But there is still much to do. The fight for accessibility doesn't end with one law or one campaign; it's an ongoing process, one that requires constant attention and action. But with Sam by my side, I'm ready for the road ahead. Together, we've travelled across the country, not just visiting football grounds but breaking down barriers and making the world a more inclusive place for everyone. And that, for me, is what this journey is ultimately about.

My passionate advocacy for promoting accessibility has naturally led me to becoming an expert in a field that is not only close to my heart but which is one of my biggest passions: football. As someone who lives and breathes the game, it has been a privilege to combine my love of football with my commitment to improving accessibility. Over the years, Sam and I have been actively involved in campaigns and initiatives aimed at making Scottish football more inclusive. But our mission didn't stop there. Our journey has taken us south of the border as well.

One of the pivotal moments in my advocacy work came in December 2021, during the height of the pandemic. I was asked to speak at AccessibAll's virtual conference. I was invited to join a panel including disabled supporters and Disability Access Officers from clubs across Europe, all coming together to share their experiences and challenges of attending football matches. As a visually impaired supporter, I had an opportunity to shed light on what it's like to navigate the world of football with a visual impairment and to attend games with a guide dog. It wasn't just about accessibility in the physical sense – things like stadium layouts or seating arrangements – but also about the cultural and emotional aspects of inclusion in football.

I discussed the highs and lows of navigating various stadiums, the different levels of support I encountered across clubs, and the ongoing need for improvement. At its core, the message I wanted to convey was that accessibility isn't a one-time fix; it's an ongoing commitment that requires dedication, empathy and awareness from every football club, big or small.

It was through my involvement in this conference that I first came into contact with the Equality, Diversity, and Inclusion (EDI) team at the English Football League (EFL). The EFL governs the three professional football divisions below the Premier League in England – the Championship, League One and League Two – and has made strides in recent years towards making football more inclusive. Their commitment to improving accessibility in football really impressed me, and I was excited when I received an invitation to speak at their Equality, Diversity and Inclusion conference at the Bescot Stadium, home of Walsall, in May 2022.

This was a huge moment for me, both personally and professionally. Speaking at the conference was an opportunity to bring attention to the issues faced by disabled supporters across English football. The conference was attended by EDI leads from various EFL clubs, and the discussions covered a wide range of topics, from race and gender equality to disability access. I was impressed by the dedication of David McArdle, the Director of Equality, Diversity & Inclusion at the EFL, and his team. Their commitment to ensuring that all EFL clubs meet high standards when it comes to equality and inclusion was clear throughout the event.

One of the cornerstones of the EFL's approach to accessibility is their EFL Together strategy. Launched with the goal of uniting clubs, supporters and communities in the fight against inequality, the strategy places a strong emphasis on making football inclusive and accessible for all. The EFL Together initiative focuses on bringing people together, regardless of their background, identity or circumstances, to celebrate the diversity that makes football such a powerful force in the world.

What I found particularly compelling about the *EFL Together* strategy is its holistic approach. It doesn't just focus on one particular group of people or one type of discrimination. Instead, it addresses a wide spectrum of issues. The EFL has set ambitious goals to increase diversity within its own staff, in club leadership positions and among its fan base. The strategy is designed to help clubs build stronger, more inclusive communities, and to ensure that everyone, no matter who, feels welcome.

A crucial part of this strategy is the EFL Code of Practice, a set of guidelines introduced to support EFL clubs in embedding best practices around equality, diversity and inclusion. The Code of Practice is not mandatory. It covers everything from recruitment practices to how clubs engage with their local communities, with a particular focus on ensuring that the needs of disabled supporters are met.

For me, the Code is one of the most progressive steps the League has taken in recent years. It's a roadmap for clubs to follow, helping them create environments that are not only compliant with the law but which are genuinely welcoming and accessible to all supporters. The Code addresses areas such as stadium facilities, including accessible seating and toilets, as well as how clubs communicate with disabled fans, making sure information is available in formats that are accessible to everyone, such as audio commentary services.

One of the key elements is the role of Disability Access Officers. Clubs that take this seriously tend to be the ones that offer the best experiences for disabled fans. Having that dedicated point of contact can make all the difference in ensuring that supporters like me feel welcome and included.

During the conference, I had the chance to meet many of these Officers, as well as EDI leads from various clubs. We shared stories, ideas and strategies for how to improve accessibility in football. What struck me was the genuine passion people had for making a difference. Many of them went above and beyond to ensure that their clubs were meeting, even exceeding the standards set out by the Code. They understand that accessibility isn't just about meeting legal obligations, it's about creating a culture of inclusion where every fan feels they belong.

Of course, while the EFL has made significant progress in recent years, there is still work to be done. Access to football matches for disabled supporters can vary widely depending on the club. Some clubs are further along in their accessibility journey, while others still have significant improvements to make. But what's clear is that the EFL is taking the issue seriously, and setting a strong example for others to follow.

It is through my work promoting accessibility in both Scotland and England that I have been able to expand my network of contacts in football, including contacts at governing bodies like the EFL and SPFL, as well as to develop relationships with key personnel at football clubs, such as the Disability Access Officers. I met Nigel, the EDI lead at Carlisle United, at the conference, and he has since become a good friend of mine as well as a colleague. In 2023 I travelled down to Carlisle United twice. The first was to experience a match day when they played Exeter City at Brunton Park, and the second a couple of months later to carry out an accessibility audit of the stadium. It was then my job to provide a report, making recommendations from infrastructure improvements to best practices in digital accessibility for the club's communications and social media pages.

Reflecting on the journey that Sam and I have taken, from attending our first football match together to speaking at the conference, I feel proud of the progress we've made, but also aware of the challenges that lie ahead. Through continued advocacy and collaboration with organisations like the EFL, I'm hopeful that we can create a future where football is inclusive for all.

At its core, my work is about more than just improving physical access – it's about changing attitudes and creating a culture where diversity is celebrated. And with initiatives like the EFL Together strategy and the EFL Code of Practice leading the way, I believe we're heading in the right direction. There's still a lot of work to be done, but Sam and I are ready for whatever comes next in this journey to make football a more inclusive and accessible game for everyone.

Chapter 13
CLOSING IN ON THE FINISH

Ground No. 30 Fir Park – Motherwell

Sam and I made our way to Fir Park on 6 July for a preseason friendly between Motherwell and Livingston. As we set off, I felt a sense of excitement building. Fir Park wasn't just another stadium to tick off our list – it was one of Scotland's oldest and most historic football grounds, steeped in tradition and brimming with memories for fans across the country. Growing up, I'd often watched games on TV that took place at Fir Park, and the sight of the old stands, the tight-knit feel of the ground and the passionate atmosphere always made an impression on me. Now, to be walking towards it with Sam by my side felt unreal.

The day began with a train ride to Glasgow, a city so familiar to me by now after many football-related adventures. From Glasgow Central, we hopped on a train to Airbles station, the closest stop to Fir Park. The journey itself was straightforward, and soon enough, we were on foot, walking the short 15-minute distance from the station to the stadium. As we approached Fir Park, the towering floodlights came into view – a sight that felt both welcoming and nostalgic.

Upon arrival, we were greeted by a friendly and helpful steward. He immediately guided us to the accessible entrance, a thoughtful gesture that saved us the usual confusion of navigating a new ground. The entrance led us directly to the accessible seating area at pitchside, giving Sam and me the perfect view of the match. It was a moment of pride and excitement – finally, we were inside one of those iconic grounds I had admired from afar for so many years.

Fir Park was originally built in 1895, and has been home to Motherwell since its inception. Nicknamed The Steelmen due to the town's industrial heritage, the club has a strong community ethos, and has been a staple of Scottish football for generations. Fir Park has a capacity of just over 13,000, which offers an intimate and electric atmosphere. Its famous East Stand, known for housing the most passionate fans, has seen countless memorable moments.

As we settled into our seats, Sam, ever the professional, lay quietly at my feet, completely at ease. Before the game kicked off, one of the accessibility stewards approached us. To my surprise, he recognised us from our social media pages. Apologetically, he informed me that the audio-descriptive commentary service wasn't available for this game – though this was something I hadn't realised Motherwell offered. The fact that they usually had such a service for visually impaired fans was a pleasant surprise. The steward invited us back for another match where the commentary would be available, promising a full match-day experience with that additional support. They even made sure Sam had a bowl of water, showing the extra level of care the club takes towards its disabled supporters.

During the game, I had the pleasure of meeting Heather, the chair of the Motherwell Disabled Supporters

Association (DSA). Her passion for improving accessibility at the club was evident as we spoke. It was heartening to hear about the strides Motherwell has made to ensure that all fans feel welcome at Fir Park. From the installation of accessible seating to the provision of audio-descriptive commentary, Motherwell is actively working to make football inclusive for everyone.

On the pitch, Motherwell looked the more dominant side throughout the game, their fluid passing and sharp attacks keeping Livingston on the back foot. By the final whistle, Motherwell had secured a 2-1 victory – a deserved win for a team that played with confidence and flair.

Leaving Fir Park that day, I felt a deep sense of satisfaction. Not only had we ticked off another ground, but we had experienced first-hand the warmth and hospitality of a club that clearly values its supporters, no matter their needs. I'm already looking forward to returning, this time to fully experience the match day with the audio-descriptive commentary in place. Fir Park had long been a ground I admired, and now, having finally visited, I can say that admiration has only deepened.

Ground No. 31 Falkirk Stadium – Falkirk

The Falkirk Stadium was a place I'd been eagerly anticipating, another important milestone in our journey. On 13 July, we finally got the chance to tick it off the list, attending a League Cup group stage game between Falkirk and my own team, Dundee United, which added an extra layer of excitement to the day. We now had quite a bit of attention on social media, and each new follower, every kind message, made the experience more special.

In the days leading up to the match, I posted on X, letting everyone know that Sam and I were heading to Falkirk. One response really stood out: a Falkirk supporter named Dawn reached out, generously offering to buy our tickets. She even went to the club shop before the game to arrange them, but when she mentioned our visit, Falkirk decided to take care of the tickets themselves. That small act of kindness speaks volumes about the club's spirit – warm, welcoming, and thoughtful.

The journey to the stadium wasn't particularly long, just a train ride to Falkirk Grahamston station followed by a short bus journey up to the stadium. But there was a sense of excitement in the air as we got closer.

Falkirk Stadium is modern, with a capacity of around 8,000, and has been home to the club since 2004. It was built after Brockville Park, the club's old home, was sold for redevelopment. Falkirk's roots run deep: the club was founded in 1876 and has long been one of the most significant teams in Scotland's lower divisions, with a passionate fan base that has seen the team through ups and downs, including a Scottish Cup win in 1957. Walking towards the stadium, I could feel that sense of history mixed with the energy of a club looking towards the future.

When we arrived, we were greeted by Murray, the club's long-serving historian and one of its most dedicated associates. Meeting Murray was a privilege. At 90 years old, he had spent decades capturing the club's history, and here he was, still devoted to the team he loved. It felt like we were in the presence of a living link to the club's past. He took us up to the boardroom, where they were celebrating Murray's birthday with cake and a small presentation. There was something very special about witnessing that; the affection and respect the club had for him was clear.

We were hosted by Graham, one of Falkirk's directors, who not only made sure we had seats in the director's box, but also made sure I had a coffee and something to eat at half-time. The thoughtfulness extended to Sam, too, who had plenty of space to settle during the game, which made everything that much easier.

The match itself ended in a 2-0 victory for Falkirk, and while it was tough to see my team, Dundee United, lose, I couldn't be too disappointed. The warmth of the Falkirk supporters, the kindness of the staff and the effort they made for Sam and me was overwhelming. As the final whistle blew, I couldn't help but feel a mixture of gratitude and pride. As has been true throughout this journey, it wasn't just about seeing football grounds, it was about the people who made each visit unique, the memories they helped to create and the moments of kindness that made all the difference. Falkirk Stadium had delivered all of that, and more.

It was another unforgettable chapter in our journey, and a reminder of the deep-rooted sense of community that football fosters. Even though the result didn't go our way, Falkirk made sure that Sam and I left with a smile on our faces and hearts full of appreciation.

Ground No. 32 East End Park – Dunfermline Athletic

By the time I began thinking about how I wanted to finish our journey, it became clear that the final destination had to be somewhere truly meaningful. As I looked over the remaining grounds, one stood out above all the rest, Forfar Athletic's Station Park. There was something poetic about ending the journey there: Forfar holds a special place in my heart because it is also home to the Guide Dogs Regional Centre for Scotland, where all guide dogs begin their formal training, including Sam. The idea of bringing our journey full circle – from where Sam started his training to completing this ambitious football adventure together – felt like the perfect ending. Station Park would be where we would complete the 42.

But before we could get to Forfar, there was another significant visit on the horizon: East End Park, home of Dunfermline Athletic. On 16 July 2024, Sam and I headed to Dunfermline for a League Cup group stage match between Dunfermline Athletic and Forfar Athletic. It was an evening game, and as I had done many times before, I shared our plans on social media. The club's Disability Access Officer, Graham, reached out, asking to give me a call to discuss our visit. This level of personal care and attention before we had even arrived was incredibly thoughtful and spoke volumes about the club.

Dunfermline Athletic, affectionately known as The Pars, is a club with a rich history. Founded in 1885, they've had moments of glory, including winning the Scottish Cup twice, in 1961 and 1968. Their home, East End Park, has hosted football matches since 1920. With a capacity of around 11,500, it's one of the more traditional grounds in Scotland, with a loyal fan base, and you can feel the weight of history when you walk into the stadium, a sense of pride and tradition that the supporters carry with them.

When Sam and I arrived at East End Park, Graham was there to meet us as promised. He guided us to a specially designated seating area for assistance dog owners, something I had never seen before at any other ground we had visited. It was a truly thoughtful touch, offering extra space for Sam and ensuring he could settle comfortably while I enjoyed the match. The simple fact that they had thought of something so specific showed just how much care had gone into making football accessible for all supporters. It was a game-changer for me: I have often encountered tight spaces at other grounds, which can make it a bit challenging for Sam.

At half-time, Graham went even further, inviting us upstairs to the club's boardroom. There we were introduced to some of the directors, and I could tell they were genuinely interested in our story. They made both Sam and me feel like honoured guests. As we stood in that boardroom, surrounded by people who had heard about our adventure and were eager to hear more, I realised just how far we had come. Sam was now at the heart of Scottish football, being celebrated by clubs, directors and supporters alike. It was unreal.

As the second half began, Graham escorted us back to the stands, where Sam had his own little space to stretch out once again. The game itself ended in a 2-0 victory for Forfar Athletic, much to the disappointment of the home crowd at East End Park. While the result might not have gone Dunfermline's way, the experience I had that evening was far from disappointing. Their kindness and commitment to accessibility were a testament to the values of Dunfermline Athletic.

I will always remember East End Park as one of the standout experiences on our journey. The game, the history of the club and the warmth of the people all combined to create something truly special. It wasn't just about ticking off another stadium on the list, it was about being part of a football community that cared. Even though the scoreline didn't favour Dunfermline that evening, the experience was another victory in this extraordinary journey Sam and I had embarked on together.

Ground No. 33 Balmoor Stadium – Peterhead

The trip to Balmoor Stadium in Peterhead was one I had been anticipating for quite some time. Peterhead is tucked away on the north-eastern coastline of Scotland, a place I had never previously ventured. We had made it as far as Aberdeen on previous journeys, but Peterhead is another 30 miles further north, perched at the edge of the North Sea. It felt like we were going to the very ends of the earth, especially considering the long trek involved. The journey from where we live was no small feat: a two-hour train ride to Aberdeen, followed by an hour-and-a-half bus journey up the coast. Yet, I knew the adventure would be worth it. There's something about discovering new places that always fills me with excitement, and this trip was no different.

Knowing the journey would be lengthy, I decided to break it up and turn it into a weekend trip. I booked a couple of nights in Aberdeen to give Sam and me some rest before and after the match. We headed up to Aberdeen the night before the game, settling into the familiar rhythm of train travel, and I found myself growing more eager as each mile passed.

The next morning, 20 July, I woke up early but not too early, around 8 a.m., and started the day with a sense of calm excitement. Sam had his breakfast and a little walk before we headed back to the hotel for mine. There's something about a hotel buffet breakfast that I always look forward to; it sets me up perfectly for the day ahead. In this particular hotel the staff were also incredibly helpful. They recognised that I might require some additional assistance at a buffet set-up, and a very kind staff member helped us to a seat and offered to go and get anything we needed. You might think that this would be common practice, but it doesn't always happen, so it always makes trips that more pleasant when it does! After a quiet and leisurely morning, we made our way to the Aberdeen bus station around midday, ready for the next leg of our journey.

The bus ride to Peterhead was smooth, and as we travelled along the coastal road, I felt that familiar sense of anticipation that comes with exploring a new town for the first time. When we finally arrived at the bus station, it was a short 15-minute walk to Balmoor Stadium, a route I'd familiarised myself with through research before we left, mostly by using Google Maps. Arriving at a new football ground, that initial glimpse of the stadium as you approach, is like a new chapter in the journey.

Balmoor Stadium, the home of Peterhead Football Club, may not have the size or grandeur of some of the bigger grounds, but it more than makes up for that with its warm, welcoming atmosphere. Peterhead, known as The Blue Toon, was founded in 1891 and has been competing in the Scottish leagues ever since. Balmoor itself is a relatively new stadium, having opened in 1997, and can hold around 3,000 fans. What it lacks in age, it certainly makes up for in character, nestled so close to the sea that you can almost taste the salt in the air.

As we arrived at the stadium, I was struck by how welcoming everyone was. One of the places highly recommended by locals was the stadium's café, which has earned a reputation for its friendly service and tasty treats. So naturally, Sam and I headed straight there before the game. It was bustling with a mix of home and away supporters, and I soon found myself with a coffee and a slice of caramel shortcake in front of me. The staff couldn't have been more accommodating; they not only helped me find a seat but even brought over a bowl of water for Sam. These are the gestures that always make me feel at ease, whether at a football ground or anywhere else. They are a reminder that Sam and I are seen, that people care and want to make us feel welcome.

Afterwards, we made our way to the accessible entrance and found our seats in the main stand. The match itself was a League Cup group stage game between Peterhead and Elgin City, and from the moment the whistle blew, it was clear we were in for an entertaining afternoon of football. The game was lively, with plenty of action and goals to keep the crowd buzzing. Peterhead's 4-2 victory over Elgin City sent the home fans into celebration mode, and it was impossible not to get swept up in the energy of the day.

As the final whistle blew, Sam and I made our way back to the bus station, and I found myself reflecting on just how much I had enjoyed the day. Balmoor Stadium may be one of the more remote grounds we've visited, but the warmth of the people and the excitement of the game made the experience memorable. The walk back to the bus station felt shorter somehow, the satisfaction of another ground ticked off the list giving me an extra spring in my step.

We arrived back in Aberdeen around 7.30 p.m., and I was thankful that I had booked another night's stay. The trip had been long and tiring, and the thought of jumping on another two-hour train back home didn't seem appealing. Instead, I grabbed a quick bite to eat and settled in for an early night, content in the knowledge that our visit to Peterhead had been another chapter in what was quickly becoming a remarkable journey across Scotland's football landscape. Balmoor Stadium, with its friendly atmosphere and picturesque location, had left a lasting impression.

Ground No. 34 Bayview Stadium – East Fife

At this stage of our journey, Sam and I had begun to build momentum. Our mission to raise awareness of the accessibility in Scottish football and to document every step of our experience at each of the 42 SPFL football grounds, was gaining ever more attention. And it wasn't just football fans who were following our story. One day, out of the blue, I received a call from STV News. They wanted to film a segment about our journey, focusing on the accessibility challenges in football and how Sam and I were breaking new ground in Scottish football history. I was thrilled at the opportunity to reach even more people, as this was a cause close to my heart. The media wasn't unfamiliar to me, either: having done campaign work in the past, I'd become quite comfortable in front of cameras, so I was more than happy to agree.

After some back and forth, we agreed that STV would join us for our upcoming visit to East Fife Football Club at Bayview Stadium. It felt like the perfect match, an iconic club with a rich history and a place that had always been known for its community spirit. Founded in 1903, East Fife has the distinction of being the only club from the lower leagues to win the Scottish Cup, which they did in 1938. Their current home, Bayview Stadium, boasts some scenic views with its location right by the Firth of Forth. The stadium, with its single stand, offers an intimate match-day experience, and the view across the water is breathtaking, especially on a clear day.

One of the key reasons for choosing this fixture, beyond the beauty of the location, was the recent opening of the Levenmouth Railway. For years, the area had been difficult to access via public transport, but the new railway station was only a 10-minute walk from Bayview, making the journey so much easier. It felt symbolic, a new line opening up to a previously underserved area, just as we were hoping to open up Scottish football to more disabled supporters.

On the evening of 23 July 2024, Sam and I set off. We caught the train to Kirkcaldy before changing for the newly opened station. It was a smooth and efficient journey, a far cry from what it might have been just a few months earlier. Arriving, I felt a sense of ease, knowing we were just a short walk away from our destination. As we approached the stadium, the STV News reporter was already waiting at the main entrance. The reporter was a familiar face, and greeted us with a warm smile. I had worked with them before when STV filmed a piece about Arbroath Football Club partnering with Guide Dogs as their charity of the year, and I knew we were in good hands.

I could feel a quiet excitement growing inside me as we filmed the introductory shots —walking up to the stadium, entering through the reception and greeting Stephen, the club's Disability Access Officer, who had kindly come out to meet us. Stephen was everything you'd want in a DAO – friendly, welcoming and deeply committed to making East Fife a club for everyone. He took us on a short tour, explaining the layout of the stadium and ensuring we were comfortable in our seats in the main stand. As we chatted, it became clear how much he cared about accessibility at the club, something that was further highlighted during our conversation about the services East Fife offered for visually impaired fans.

The most surprising moment came when Stephen handed me an audio-descriptive commentary headset. I had no idea that East Fife, a League Two side, provided this service. Stephen explained that it had been introduced at the request of a visually impaired fan, and that he delivered the commentary at every home game. It was genuinely moving to hear him speak so passionately about the importance of making football accessible and experience the effort he and the club had put in to cater to disabled fans. It's rare to see such a service at this level of the game, and it spoke volumes about the club's commitment to inclusivity.

We continued filming, with STV capturing Stephen's explanation of his role at the club and how East Fife had taken steps to ensure match days were accessible for all. It was a proud moment for both of us, highlighting not just our journey but the wider message we were trying to spread – that football should be for everyone, regardless of ability.

The match itself was a high-scoring affair, East Fife comfortably defeating Brechin City 4-0 in this League Cup group stage game. Bayview may be small, but it was buzzing with excitement as the home side secured a convincing win. Throughout the match, I tuned into Stephen's commentary and was impressed by the level of detail and his enthusiasm; it added a new layer to my experience as a visually impaired supporter, one that I wished more clubs would embrace.

As the final whistle blew and the crowd began to disperse, I walked with Sam back to the train station. I felt a deep sense of fulfilment, not just from ticking off another ground on our list but from the positive experiences we'd had at East Fife. The people, the atmosphere, the accessibility, it all left a lasting impression. This was what football should be about: inclusion, community and passion.

When we boarded the train back to Kirkcaldy, I couldn't help but smile. Every visit brought us closer to our goal, but more importantly, it was proving that with a little effort, football can become more accessible to everyone. East Fife had shown that even smaller clubs can lead the way in making the game more inclusive, and for that, I will always have a special place in my heart for Bayview Stadium.

Chapter 14
MOMENTS BEFORE THE FINAL WHISTLE

Ground No. 35 Rugby Park – Kilmarnock

Two days after our memorable trip to Bayview Stadium, Sam and I found ourselves boarding a train down to Ayrshire. Our destination was Rugby Park in Kilmarnock for an exhilarating Europa League play-off tie. Kilmarnock, or Killie as the fans fondly call them, would face off against the Belgian Pro League side Cercle Brugge in front of crowds brimming with anticipation. There was something in the air, a sense that this was more than just another game. It felt like a momentous occasion, not just for Kilmarnock but for Sam and me as well.

I had been in touch with the club earlier in the week and reached out to Lochlin, Kilmarnock's media officer, who graciously granted us media accreditation. The idea of sitting on the accessible platform at a sold-out Rugby Park, watching Kilmarnock compete for European glory, was thrilling. The club was founded in 1869, making it one of the oldest football clubs in Scotland, while Rugby Park itself has been the club's home since 1899, and despite numerous renovations, the ground still retains a unique charm. The club has long been a cornerstone of the Kilmarnock community, and tonight, the entire town seemed united in their support.

I had also connected with Laurie, a Kilmarnock fan I met online. He is a passionate supporter who hosts a radio show for the local hospital as well as being a co-host on the SFF Podcast. He invited me to be interviewed about my travels with Sam and our experiences in Scottish football after the game, an opportunity I was excited to accept. There was something special about sharing our story in front of the online community that had been such a significant part of my journey.

As the train pulled into Kilmarnock station, we disembarked and began the short 15–20 minute walk to Rugby Park. The streets were alive with supporters, many of them draped in blue and white scarves, flags hung proudly from windows, and banners celebrating this rare European night fluttered in the breeze. You could feel the buzz of excitement ripple through the town. As we neared the stadium, that energy only intensified, a collective belief that perhaps, just perhaps, tonight would be a night to remember.

At the stadium's main reception, I collected the audio-descriptive commentary headset, grateful that Kilmarnock were ensuring accessibility for all fans. I always appreciate clubs that took these additional steps, and this was something I wanted to highlight in my own journey. Just before heading to the media entrance, Laurie arrived with his father. It was good to meet him in person after all our online interactions. Laurie is a wheelchair user, and would be sitting on the accessible platform with Sam and me.

We entered Rugby Park through the media entrance,

and I felt a thrill as I collected my media pass, a reminder that this journey had opened doors for me, both literally and figuratively. Lochlin greeted us warmly and showed us to the accessible platform behind the goal, where we had a perfect view of the pitch. Rugby Park was buzzing, with the stands packed to capacity, and the visiting Cercle Brugge fans had turned out in full force, creating a lively, competitive atmosphere.

The match itself was gripping. Kilmarnock, buoyed by the home crowd, played with heart and determination. Despite the nerves of playing on the European stage, they matched Brugge stride for stride. At half-time, Lochlin came down to the accessible platform with one of Kilmarnock's famous pies for me to try. Now, I had heard all the hype about these pies, and I can confirm they live up to it! Crispy, warm and filled with hearty goodness, perfect fuel for the second half!

The match was hard-fought but ended in a 1-1 draw, leaving everything to play for in the second leg in Belgium. For me, it wasn't just the result that stood out, it was the entire experience. From the sense of belonging in the packed stadium to meeting Laurie and his father, it was one of those nights in football that stays with you long after the final whistle.

After the game, as the stadium slowly emptied, Laurie interviewed me for his hospital radio show. His questions were thoughtful and well-researched, and it was clear how much he cared about Kilmarnock and its community. When I listened back to the broadcast a few days later, I was struck by his professionalism and the connection we had made through this shared love of the game.

Before long, Laurie and his father offered us a lift back

to Kilmarnock station. As Sam and I settled into the train home, I couldn't help but reflect on what an incredible evening it had been. Another European night, another ground conquered – but more importantly, another chance to share in the passion and joy that football brings to so many.

Ground No. 36 New Dundas Park – Bonnyrigg Rose

Bonnyrigg Rose Athletic Football Club, a name immersed in tradition yet relatively new to the professional ranks of Scottish football, caught my attention when they were promoted to the SPFL in 2022. Rising from the Lowland League, they quickly established themselves as a credible force, while their modest ground, New Dundas Park, now hosted competitive league matches. Bonnyrigg's success represented more than just football, it symbolised the perseverance and community spirit of this small Edinburgh suburb. I was keen to experience the match-day atmosphere at one of the smallest football grounds in the SPFL, and Saturday, 27 July 2024 provided the perfect opportunity.

The journey to Bonnyrigg began with a familiar routine: a train from Perth to Haymarket station, one of Edinburgh's main transport hubs, and then a bus down to Bonnyrigg, nestled just southeast of the capital. Sam and I had been on many adventures together, but something about this trip felt different. Perhaps it was the intimate nature of New Dundas Park or the local charm Bonnyrigg Rose exuded as a community club. There's a certain magic about smaller grounds like this, a reminder that football isn't just about big stadiums and flashy lights but about people, passion and a deep connection to the local area.

New Dundas Park is the beating heart of Bonnyrigg. With a capacity of just over 2,000, it seems humble compared to the grand arenas of Scottish football, but what it lacks in size, it makes up for in character. From its open terracing to the sense of community pride that reverberates throughout the town, it's a throwback to a time when football was more about camaraderie and less about commercialisation. As we arrived, the non-league vibes were immediately apparent: the ground had an authenticity that larger, more polished stadiums can sometimes lack. Despite its size, Bonnyrigg Rose has been working hard to make New Dundas Park more accessible for all fans, and I was pleased to see that they had a few dedicated wheelchair spaces.

Sam and I walked around the perimeter of the ground, taking in the sights and sounds of match day. It's mostly terracing, with a few dedicated seats in a small stand, basic but perfectly fitting for a club like Bonnyrigg Rose, whose ethos is grounded in grassroots football. While I was contemplating where we'd settle in to watch the game, we bumped into a familiar face: Paul, the commercial manager at Arbroath. He recognised us from a previous meeting at the Guide Dogs Regional Centre in Forfar the year before, when Arbroath had taken Guide Dogs as their charity partner. It was good to reconnect with him, and he invited us to sit in the dedicated seated area, close to where the Arbroath communications team were stationed and reporting on the match.

As we settled into our seats, the sense of community between both sets of supporters was palpable. This match, part of the League Cup group stage, wasn't for high stakes, as neither Bonnyrigg nor Arbroath had a chance to progress.

Still, there was something special about the occasion. The fans, many of whom had probably followed Bonnyrigg Rose from their non-league days, were passionate, proudly donning their team's red and white scarves and filling the modest terraces with a quiet but determined optimism. I imagined what it must feel like for them, watching their team fight for recognition on the professional stage after years of competing in the lower leagues.

At half-time, it was time to explore one of my favourite aspects of Scottish football: the pies. New Dundas Park's pie hut offered a variety of options, and I couldn't resist trying the Buffalo Chicken pie. Now, I've had my fair share of pies on this journey across the 42 SPFL grounds, and this one ranked up there as one of the best. It was bursting with flavour, the pastry perfectly flaky and the spicy kick from the buffalo sauce adding a satisfying twist. Sam, as always, didn't miss out on the half-time festivities. I made sure to bring along some biscuits for him, and he happily crunched away on his half-time bone, tail wagging contentedly.

The second half of the game unfolded in much the same way as the first, relatively uneventful but not without its charms. Both teams fought hard, but it was clear that the result didn't hold much significance for either. Arbroath did, however, manage to snatch a late goal in the dying minutes of the game, securing a 1-0 win. It wasn't the most thrilling match I'd witnessed, but that didn't matter. What made the day memorable was the entire experience, and the chance to visit a new ground.

As the final whistle blew, Sam and I lingered, soaking in the atmosphere before making our way back to the bus stop. It was a short walk down the street, where we caught the bus back to Edinburgh city centre to catch our train home. Despite the quiet nature of the game itself, this trip to Bonnyrigg Rose felt meaningful in its own way.

For the club, promotion to the SPFL wasn't just a sporting achievement, it was a victory for everyone who had supported them throughout their journey. New Dundas Park might be one of the smallest grounds in the league, but it has a big heart, much like the club and its loyal fans.

As Sam and I headed home, I felt grateful for yet another positive experience, one that reminded me of the power of football to bring people together, no matter the size of the stadium or the stakes.

Ground No. 37 Links Park – Montrose

The excitement in the air was palpable as the opening weekend of the 2024/25 SPFL league campaign arrived. For football fans, there's something special about the start of a new season. It brings renewed hope, fresh ambitions and the promise of unpredictable twists and turns. For Sam and me, it also meant another step closer to our personal goal: visiting all 42 SPFL grounds. With just a few left, I found myself poring over the fixture list, debating which match to attend on the Saturday. And then, the obvious choice struck me: Links Park, home of Montrose Football Club, was calling.

Montrose Football Club, nicknamed The Gable Endies, was founded way back in 1879. Nestled on the edge of the North Sea, the coastal town of Montrose has always embraced its football club as a source of local pride. Links Park, where the club plays its home games, is one of those smaller grounds with real character, the kind of place where you can sense the history in every corner. With a capacity of just over 4,900, it's an intimate setting, but that's part of what makes it so special.

So, on Saturday, 3 August, Sam and I jumped on the train, eager to see Montrose kick off their League One campaign against Kelty Hearts. There's something calming about train journeys, especially with Sam by my side. We had our usual routine: he settled comfortably by my feet, and I spent the ride thinking about the day ahead. It wasn't long before we were approached by Marc, a fellow passenger who recognised us from social media. It was always heartening to meet people who were following our journey.

Marc, as it turned out, was also heading to the match. He worked with the BBC, covering football games, mostly down south, but he was up in Scotland for the weekend to catch the highly anticipated Dundee derby the following day, a fixture Sam and I were also planning to attend. Even better, Marc is also a fellow Dundee United supporter, which made for easy conversation. We spent much of the train journey talking about football, our shared love for the game and the unique experiences that come with following Scottish football. It was one of those moments that reminded me why I loved this journey so much.

Upon arriving in Montrose, we decided to grab some lunch before heading to the game. Montrose itself is a charming coastal town, known for its rich maritime history and picturesque scenery. We found a little café in the town centre, where Marc insisted on paying for our lunch.

Links Park is a ground that perfectly reflects the character of Montrose, modest but full of heart. The stadium, originally opened in 1887, has undergone several renovations over the years, including the installation of an artificial pitch in 2015, which allows the club to host community events and maintain a top-class surface year-round. The ground is mostly terracing, with one large, single-tiered stand that offers great views of the action. As we approached the entrance, a helpful steward immediately recognised the need for accessibility and showed Sam and me to the accessible entrance, a small but significant gesture that always makes a difference on days like these.

Once inside, we made our way to the terracing behind the goal. I've always had a fondness for terracing; there's something about standing alongside fellow fans, immersed in the atmosphere, that feels more connected to the soul of football. Sam and I settled in, ready for the game to begin. It wasn't the most thrilling of matches, but I found myself captivated by the Montrose supporters. Despite the small size of the town and the club, the fans were passionate, vocal and unwavering in their support. You could sense the pride they felt in their team, the kind of pride that comes from years of standing by them through thick and thin.

The match itself ended in a 1-1 draw. Both Montrose and Kelty Hearts fought hard, but this was the first match of the season and neither team seemed too eager to risk it all. For the Gable Endies, it was a solid enough start to the new campaign, and the draw left both sides with a point to build on. As the final whistle blew, I couldn't help but feel a sense of satisfaction. The football season was officially back, and with it came all the hope, anticipation and possibility that makes it so addictive.

As we made our way back to Montrose railway station, I reflected on how close we were to achieving our goal. Links Park was now ticked off the list, bringing us one step closer. But beyond the tick, I left Montrose with a deeper appreciation for the club and the town. It may not be the biggest club in Scotland, but they're a club with heart, and that's what football is all about.

Sam and I boarded the train home, feeling the familiar contentment that comes after another successful day of football. I glanced at Sam, curled up at my feet, and couldn't help but smile. We were getting closer to the end of this incredible journey, but in many ways, it felt like we were just getting started. I knew that no matter how many grounds we visited, every new experience would bring something special, just like Montrose had.

Ground No. 38 Palmerston Park – Queen of the South

As Sam and I approached the final stretch of our mission to visit all 42 SPFL grounds, I found myself reflecting more and more on the journey. With fewer than a handful of grounds left to tick off, each new stadium carried a deeper significance. By this point, it was about savouring the moments, the stories, and the connections that came with every trip. Our final ground, I had already decided, would be Station Park in Forfar on 21 September for their League Two match against Stranraer. But before that grand finale, we still had a few more to visit, including one of the furthest away, Queen of the South Football Club, situated down in Dumfries near the Scottish border.

Queen of the South, affectionately known as The Doonhamers, dates back to 1919. Their home, Palmerston Park, is one of Scotland's more unique football grounds, with character in abundance, much like the town of Dumfries itself. Palmerston Park, with a capacity of around 8,500, is famed for its mixture of old-school charm and community spirit, making it a place I was eager to experience first-hand.

For this visit, I decided to attend a local derby, a fixture between Queen of the South and their nearby rivals Annan Athletic. On 17 August, Sam and I boarded the train to Glasgow before catching a connection to Dumfries. There was something about train journeys like this that made the experience feel like an adventure, a journey not just across the Scottish landscape, but deeper into the heart of the country's football culture.

Adding to the occasion, my good friend Nigel, who lives in Carlisle, was going to join us for the match. Nigel and I had bonded over our mutual love for the game, and sharing these moments with friends made them even more memorable. When we arrived in Dumfries, we had some time before kick-off, so we wandered through the town centre, soaking in the atmosphere of this historic border town. Dumfries is rich in history, with connections to Robert Burns, and it's known for its close-knit community, a trait I would soon come to associate with Queen of the South as well.

Ahead of the game, I posted on X about our upcoming visit to Palmerston Park, mentioning that it was part of our journey to complete all 42 SPFL grounds. To my surprise, Dan, CEO of Queen of the South, reached out. He called and expressed how much he was looking forward to welcoming Sam and me to the club. His gesture showed just how much Queen of the South valued their supporters and visitors.

When we arrived at Palmerston Park, Dan himself met us outside the stadium, which meant a lot. But what really touched me was the gift he had for Sam – a Queen of the South dog bandana. It reinforced what I had come to love about Scottish football, the genuine warmth and generosity of the people we met along the way.

Dan gave us a brief tour of the ground before leading us to our seats in the main stand. Palmerston Park, with its wooden seats in certain sections and standing terraces, exudes a nostalgic charm that you rarely find in modern stadiums. There is something raw and authentic about it, something that makes you feel connected to the history of the club and its supporters. This is a place that holds memories for generations of fans.

The game itself was an entertaining affair. Derby matches always have an extra layer of intensity, and this one was no different. Queen of the South were determined to put on a show for their home fans, and the energy in the stands was electric. Annan Athletic, their rivals from just a short distance away, fought hard, but Queen of the South's quality shone through. The Doonhamers secured a 2-0 victory, sending the home crowd into rapturous applause. It was the kind of game that reminded me why I loved football so much, not just for the skill on the pitch, but for the passion and pride that radiates from the stands.

Sharing this experience with Nigel made it even more special. He and I had attended a few games together over the years, but there was something unique about this one, knowing that we were nearing the end of our journey. Nigel had always been a supportive friend, and the fact that he would also be joining us at our final ground in Forfar in a few weeks' time made me appreciate our friendship even more.

As the final whistle blew, and we made our way out of Palmerston Park, I couldn't help but feel a sense of gratitude. Queen of the South had welcomed us with open arms, and I left with fond memories of both the match and the people we met. Sam, as always, had been the star of the day, wearing his new bandana with pride.

The quest to visit all 42 SPFL grounds had brought us to places like Dumfries, where football wasn't just a game but a way of life. As Sam and I boarded the train back home, I felt a renewed sense of purpose. We were so close to achieving our goal, but more than that, we were collecting stories that I would carry with me for the rest of my life. Each ground was more than just a tick on the list; it was another reminder of the beauty of Scottish football, where clubs like Queen of the South make you feel like part of their family.

Ground No. 39 SMISA Stadium – St Mirren

St Mirren is a name that carries a deep history in Scottish football, one intertwined with legendary figures, like Sir Alex Ferguson, who managed the club from 1974 to 1978. Long before he cemented his legacy at Aberdeen and went on to become the iconic manager of Manchester United, Ferguson was cutting his teeth in Paisley, leading St Mirren to the First Division title in 1977. It's strange to think that this small club helped shape the early career of a man who would go on to change football forever.

On 14 September 2024, Sam and I made our way to Paisley for the Scottish Premiership clash between St Mirren and Kilmarnock. It was a trip I had been looking forward to for some time, knowing how much history this club held, not just because of Sir Alex but because of its deep roots in Scottish football. I could feel the significance of the day building as we boarded the train from Glasgow to Paisley. The journey was easy, just a quick ride from

Glasgow Central to Paisley St James, a station conveniently located right next to St Mirren's home ground, the SMISA Stadium. In terms of accessibility via public transport, it's one of the most straightforward trips to make in Scottish football, which was a relief.

But as I made that journey, my mind wandered back to the club's former home, Love Street. Love Street was where St Mirren played for 115 years, from 1894 until 2009, when the club moved to the newly built SMISA Stadium. I'd heard many stories about the old ground, a place that held countless memories for generations of fans. With a capacity of over 10,000, Love Street was known for its passionate atmosphere. Love Street was where St Mirren won the 1987 Scottish Cup and where they saw great moments of triumph and heartbreak. However, like many clubs, the financial pressures of maintaining such an old ground led to the decision to move. In 2009, the club left behind Love Street's history and charm to enter a new era at the SMISA Stadium, a more modern facility with state-of-the-art amenities, better suited for the club's future. While the move was undoubtedly a practical one, the nostalgia for Love Street lingers among older supporters who grew up with the rickety stands and tightly packed terraces.

As we arrived at the SMISA Stadium, those thoughts of history gave way to the excitement of the present. The stadium, built in 2009 and with a capacity of just over 8,000, is sleek and modern. Named after the St Mirren Independent Supporters Association (SMISA), it is a testament to the community spirit of the club and its fans. There is something welcoming about the place, and that feeling only deepened when I met James, the club's Media Officer, who had been in touch with me leading up to the match.

He had arranged media accreditation for Sam and me, as well as access to the audio-descriptive commentary.

It was clear that St Mirren, like so many of the clubs we had visited, valued the fan experience, especially when it came to accessibility. We were shown to our seats on the accessible platform in the main stand. The platform was situated at the back, offering a perfect view of the pitch while allowing Sam the space to comfortably settle. What I found particularly impressive was the ease of access: there's a doorway that leads directly from the supporters' bar onto the platform, making it convenient for fans who want to grab a drink or snack before the game without having to navigate too far. It's these little touches that make a big difference.

As we settled into our seats, James popped over to say hello and to make sure everything was working smoothly with the commentary headset. I was immediately struck by how thoughtful and well-prepared the staff at St Mirren were. It was clear that accessibility was not an afterthought here, it was woven into the fabric of how the club operated. I had everything and we felt genuinely valued as a supporter.

The game itself was exciting. St Mirren and Kilmarnock played out a 2-2 draw, though the match would become notorious for a few controversial VAR decisions that had fans and pundits talking for days and weeks afterward. As I sat there, listening to the commentary and taking in the action, I was reminded once again of how far football has come, not just in terms of technology but in how clubs are now striving to be more inclusive and accessible. I found myself immersed in the game, appreciating the passion of the fans around me and the atmosphere that filled the stadium.

As the final whistle blew and we made our way back to Paisley St James to catch our train home, I realised that, in just one week, we would be setting off for Forfar to visit our final ground, No. 42 out of 42. The thought was almost overwhelming. Years ago, the idea of completing this journey had felt like a distant dream, something that seemed impossible. Yet here we were, one step away achieving that dream.

As Sam and I boarded the train, I couldn't help but think back to all the places we had been, all the people we had met along the way. The journey wasn't just about football, it was about the connections we made, the stories we heard and the moments that would stay with me forever. St Mirren, with its rich history and welcoming spirit, had become a part of that story, and I was grateful.

Chapter 15
YOU'LL NEVER WALK ALONE

Ground No. 40 Celtic Park – Celtic

Celtic Park holds a special place in my heart, and on our incredible journey Celtic Football Club have been one of the most supportive clubs of the 42, and of our mission to highlight the important accessibility work being done across all clubs in Scotland, so it's only fitting they that they get their own chapter in this book.

Among the many football grounds Sam and I have visited, Celtic Park stands out not only for its grand scale and electric atmosphere but for the warmth and care we've always received there. The team at Celtic Park, particularly Alexis Dobbin, the Disability Access Officer, have always ensured that our visits are as smooth and enjoyable as possible. Alexis's dedication to making sure that every disabled supporter, whether cheering for Celtic or the opposition, has the best possible experience is phenomenal. Her attention to detail and commitment to accessibility have made every trip to Celtic Park feel like a homecoming, where Sam and I are not just visitors but valued guests.

I've been to Celtic Park many times since around 2008,

often with my brother who is a massive Celtic fan. When we were younger, we would go to games there every so often. One match that stands out was a Champions League qualifier against Arsenal, shortly after Tony Mowbray became Celtic manager. There's nothing quite like the atmosphere at Celtic Park on a Champions League night, the roar of the Champions League anthem, 60,000 fans belting out 'You'll Never Walk Alone', and the eruption of the crowd when Celtic score. It's an experience that stays with you forever.

A few weeks before that Arsenal game, my brother and I were in London for the Wembley Cup, a preseason tournament in which Celtic were playing. As a birthday present for him, I'd bought tickets to see them face Egyptian giants Al-Ahly and Tottenham Hotspur. I remember arriving at Wembley for the Spurs game, and my brother placing what felt like the most ridiculous bet: Celtic to win 2-0, with Chris Killen scoring the first goal. The odds were crazy because no one would've expected that outcome.

But minutes into the first half, Chris Killen fired in the opener for Celtic. I've never seen anyone celebrate a goal quite like my brother did that day! Later, Georgios Samaras scored a second, and Celtic won 2-0. My brother was over the moon, not just because Celtic had won, but because his unlikely bet had just earned him a few hundred quid.

That weekend was made even more special by the chance to watch Pep Guardiola's Barcelona team in action again, with players like Lionel Messi showcasing their brilliance. To top it off, Celtic went on to win the Wembley Cup, making the entire trip one of the most unforgettable weekends we've ever had.

Celtic Football Club is more than just a football team; it's a institution deeply woven into the fabric of Scottish and

Irish culture. Founded in 1888 with strong Irish roots, the club has always stood as a symbol of pride and identity for many. One of the most remarkable chapters in their history came in 1967 when Celtic became the first British team to win the European Cup, now known as the Champions League. This victory, achieved by a squad forever known as the Lisbon Lions, came against the formidable Inter Milan and is etched in the history books. The Lisbon Lions' triumph was a symbol of hope and achievement for their fans. I consider myself incredibly fortunate to have seen this very European Cup in the trophy cabinet in Celtic Park's trophy cabinet in the boardroom. It's a humbling reminder of the club's glorious past and their ongoing legacy.

Sam and I visited Celtic Park on three separate occasions as part of our journey to visit all 42 Scottish football grounds. But what makes our visits to Celtic Park even more special is the unique reason we've returned more than once: to support the Celtic Women's team, which has played a pioneering role in Scottish football. Celtic Football Club became the first club in Scotland to offer audio-descriptive commentary at women's games, a service that had previously been available only for men's matches. This milestone is a testament to Celtic's commitment to inclusivity and equal access for all fans.

Callum, Katie and Kevin provide the audio-descriptive commentary at Celtic. I have been fortunate to get to know them, and that's the great thing about the audio-descriptive commentary service, not just at Celtic but across other grounds that provide this service too: you get to know the commentators and form friendships at games with other people at the clubs and also other supporters who are using the service too. Katie has provided the commentary at every

Celtic woman's home games that Sam and I have attended and does a fantastic job every time. She is often joined by Callum, a man I first met in 2021 at Tannadice when he came to a Dundee United v Celtic game to join the audio-descriptive commentary team.

I must also give a special mention to the amazing accessibility stewards at Celtic as well: Nicola and Evelyn, who are both superstars. I first met Nicola when Sam and I were invited as guests by Celtic to the Celtic Women v Hibernian on the final day of the 23/24 SWPL season, where a victory would secure Celtic their first ever League title. Nicola provides invaluable support and is a natural pro. She ensured that the audio-descriptive commentary headset was working okay, supported us when navigating the ground and helped us to and from our seats before and after the game and also at half-time. I have since met Nicola several times, and she goes above and beyond on match days to support visually impaired fans; she is a real credit to the club and one of the unsung heroes at Celtic. Nicola is now someone that Sam and I are honoured to call a friend. Evelyn has also been a great support when Sam and I have attended women's games at Airdrie, where the team previously played the majority of their home matches before moving to New Douglas Park in Hamilton. Evelyn is a long-standing member of the Celtic accessibility team and has a wealth of knowledge about stadium accessibility. She also goes out of her way to provide invaluable support to disabled fans on a match day.

The first Celtic Women's match we attended with this groundbreaking service was a resounding 5-0 victory over Hearts at Celtic Park on 21 April 2024. I still remember the thrill of that day, not just because of the match itself but because of the way Sam and I were treated. The team at Celtic Park made sure that our experience was nothing short of exceptional. We were provided with a comfortable padded seat and a headset for the audio-descriptive commentary, and were even treated to a half-time pie and access to the bar before the game. It was a day filled with joy, both on and off the pitch, and it left an indelible mark.

The significance of this achievement for women's football in Scotland was something I was eager to promote on social media, and it was heartening to see how many people celebrated this milestone. Recognising the importance of what they had accomplished, Celtic invited Sam and me to the final game of the season against Hibernian Women as guests in their boardroom. We were welcomed into the boardroom and introduced to some of the incredible staff who work behind the scenes to make Celtic Park the iconic place it is. Alexis Dobbin introduced us to Brendan Rodgers, the manager of the Celtic men's team. Meeting Brendan was an honour, especially since his team had just clinched the league title the previous day at Celtic Park!

That day concluded in dramatic fashion, with Amy Gallacher scoring a late goal to secure a 1-0 victory for Celtic Women over Hibernian, a win that sealed the League title for the first time in the history of the Celtic Women's team. To witness such a historic moment in person, to be there as the final whistle blew and the celebrations began, was beyond words. The victory on the pitch was also a triumph for the progress of women's football in Scotland and a testament to the club's commitment to making football accessible to everyone.

Being present for such an event, in a place that has always welcomed us with open arms, made me realise just how much Celtic Park means to me. It's not just one of my favourite grounds; it's a place where Sam and I have felt truly included and where memories have been made that will last a lifetime.

Chapter 16
BLACK & TANGERINE

Ground No. 41 Tannadice Park – Dundee United

I deliberately left talking about Tannadice Park and Dundee United until near the end of this book. It felt only right to give the stadium and the club that has meant so much to me, and to Sam, its own dedicated chapter. For me, Tannadice is more than a football ground; it's home. It's the place where some of my best memories have been made, where the highs of joy and the lows of heartache have helped shaped my love for football. More than any other stadium, Tannadice has been a constant. The atmosphere, the familiar hum of the crowd and the sea of tangerine all form a sensory experience that goes far beyond watching a game. This is the place where Sam and I truly belong. The familiar faces we see every other week in the stands, the friendly and welcoming club staff and stewards, the people who sit around us where we sit for each home game, and the fantastic audio-descriptive commentary from Stuart and Sam make coming to Dundee United home games something I look forward to every other week.

Dundee United Football Club itself has history that has resonated deeply with me over the years. Originally founded in 1909 as Dundee Hibernian, the club was created to represent the Irish Catholic community in Dundee, though it quickly became a symbol of the whole city. In 1923, the club changed its name to Dundee United, marking a shift in identity and opening its doors to a broader fan base. Since then, United has experienced everything from the lows of relegation to the highs of European glory.

Tannadice Park has been home to the club since its earliest days, and it too has evolved over the years. Located on Tannadice Street in Dundee, the stadium sits in a unique position, just a stone's throw from the home of our rivals, Dundee. You could stand on the pavement outside Tannadice and toss a football to someone standing outside Dens Park. The close proximity of the two stadiums has only fuelled the fierce rivalry between the clubs, and the Dundee derby is one of the most passionate and competitive in Scottish football.

Tannadice itself is steeped in history. The ground has undergone several redevelopments, yet it has always retained that intimate, old-school football feel. Originally a small, modest stadium, Tannadice gradually expanded to accommodate Dundee United's growing success. In 1962, the West Stand was constructed. Nicknamed The Shed, it quickly became the heart and soul of the stadium. It's where I found myself for many matches, including my very first game, one that remains vivid in my memory: a preseason friendly against Pep Guardiola's Barcelona.

That game was my first experience at Tannadice. It was a warm summer's day, and I was there with my younger brother. We took our seats in The Shed, the area renowned for its passionate supporters, and from the moment we sat down, the atmosphere was electric. Barcelona, a footballing powerhouse, were in town, bringing with them some of the biggest names in world football. Yet, despite the star-studded opposition, there was a sense of hope and belief in the air, as if anything could happen on that hallowed ground.

And then, it did. I'll never forget the eruption of noise that echoed through Tannadice when Prince Buaben scored the opening goal for Dundee United. The Shed was rocking, and for those few seconds, it felt as though we were on top of the world. It didn't matter that it was a friendly match, or that Barcelona would eventually go on to win. In that moment, United had the upper hand, and the crowd, myself included, basked in the glory. That was the moment when I fell in love with the club.

Over the years, Tannadice has been the setting for countless more moments like that, some joyous, some heartbreaking. From United winning the Scottish Premier Division title in 1983 under legendary manager Jim McLean, to the team reaching the semi-finals of the European Cup in 1984, Tannadice has been home to some of the greatest achievements in Scottish football. Even during the tough times, when United faced relegation battles or disappointing seasons, Tannadice remained a place of hope and belief.

For Sam and me, Tannadice is a place of comfort. Of the 42 SPFL grounds across Scotland, none compare to this one. The familiarity of the surroundings, the warmth of the fans and the unwavering support for the team create an experience that is unlike any other. The club has given me so many cherished memories, and yes, it's also caused its fair share of heartache. But that's what football is, isn't it? A rollercoaster of emotions that we willingly ride, time and time again, because the love for the club outweighs the pain of defeat.

In more recent years, as I started attending Dundee United games more regularly with Sam by my side, those matches, both home and away, have provided some of my most cherished memories in football. Every game felt like part of a larger story, woven together by the highs and lows of following a club like Dundee United. Football is often more than just the 90 minutes on the pitch; it's about the build-up, the atmosphere and the shared experiences with those around you. For me, it's also about the bond I have with Sam, who has been a constant presence on this journey. Together, we've experienced moments that will stay with me for a lifetime, and two games stand out.

The first is our Europa Conference League qualifier against AZ Alkmaar on 4 August 2022. That night was special from the moment I arrived at Tannadice. There's something magical about European nights, the sense that you're part of something bigger, that your club is stepping onto the continental stage, facing teams from leagues we don't regularly encounter. You can feel it in the air: the tension, the excitement, the anticipation. As I sat in the stands with Sam, I could hear the familiar chants echoing around the ground, the energy in the crowd building as the game got underway.

We weren't just playing any team; AZ Alkmaar is a club with pedigree. Yet, Dundee United came out with confidence and resilience. The moment that truly made the night unforgettable was Glenn Middleton's goal. It started with a moment of brilliance from Dylan Levitt, who picked out Middleton with a long, sweeping switch of play. I could hear the crowd collectively rise as Middleton controlled the ball. In that split second, time seemed to slow. Every touch, every movement felt magnified, as if the entire stadium was holding its breath. Then Middleton, beating the Alkmaar defender, let fly, and the ball hit the back of the net. The roar from the Tannadice crowd was deafening. The stands erupted in a way I hadn't felt in years, pure, unfiltered joy. I remember hugging the people around me, total strangers united in this shared moment of ecstasy.

It wasn't just about the goal; it was what it symbolised. For Dundee United, a win like that on a European night was more than just a result. It was a statement, a reminder that we could still compete on the big stage, that Tannadice could still be the fortress it once was. Even though the second leg in Alkmaar would be a different story, that 1-0 victory at home remains etched in my memory as one of the best nights I've experienced as a fan.

The other standout memory takes me to the Highlands, to Ross County's Victoria Park, for the final game of the 2021/22 season. Dundee United went into that game knowing we had a shot at securing fourth place in the league, which would mean European qualification. It was one of those games where the significance was felt long before kick-off. The Dundee United faithful travelled in numbers, and the away end was packed with tangerine. There was a carnival-like atmosphere, with inflatable beach balls bouncing through the crowd, songs being sung louder with every passing minute, and that infectious sense of belief that maybe, just maybe, we could finish the season on a high.

Ross County may not have the stature of a Celtic or Rangers, but they're never an easy opponent, especially at home. The game was tense, but we played with grit and determination. Every pass, every tackle felt like a step closer to Europe. When the final whistle blew and we had secured a 2-1 win, the entire away end erupted. There was an outpouring of relief, joy and pride that we had done it; we had finished fourth, and European football was coming back to Tannadice. I remember looking down at Sam, who was as calm as ever amid the chaos, and feeling this overwhelming sense of accomplishment. We had been on this journey together, and to end the season on such a high was an incredible feeling.

Then came the inevitable pitch invasion. It's something that often divides opinion, but in that moment, it felt like the perfect release of all the pent-up emotion from a rollercoaster season. Fans streamed onto the pitch, hugging players, taking in the moment, basking in the glory of what had just been achieved. I didn't join the invasion, but I stood back, soaking in the scene, feeling that collective joy sweep through the away end. It was one of those rare moments when it all comes together, when the love for your club, the effort of the players, and the passion of the fans align in perfect harmony.

Those two games, the night we beat AZ Alkmaar at Tannadice and the away day at Ross County, are etched in my memory not just because of the results but because of the emotions they stirred. They remind me of why I love this club, of the ups (and downs) that make following Dundee United such a unique experience. Through it all, Sam has been by my side, experiencing every high and low, and those memories are even more special because we've shared them together.

Tannadice will always be home for Sam and me. And no matter where our journey takes us next, this stadium, and this club, will forever hold a special place in our hearts.

Top 5 Favourite Grounds

I'm often asked about my favourite grounds in the 42. The list is very difficult to narrow down. They are all amazing in their own unique way, and every club has been so welcoming and supportive to both me and Sam, but here are the ones that we both loved visiting:

1. Celtic Park – A fabulous venue to watch football with an incredible match-day accessibility team

2. Tannadice – The stadium Sam and I have visited the most and the one we call home

3. Galabank – Home of Annan Athletic, some great modern facilities and a really great community club

4. Borough Briggs – Home of Elgin City, an old school football ground that has real character

5. Fir Park – Home of Motherwell, a club with a great Disabled Supporters Association and truly dedicated to accessibility

Chapter 17
FULL TIME – 42/42

Ground No. 42 Station Park – Forfar

My alarm went off early, around 7.00 a.m., pulling me from the restless sleep of the night before. As I fumbled for my phone to silence it, the date on my phone screen stared back at me: Saturday, 21 September 2024. It wasn't just any Saturday, though, it was *the* Saturday. A day I had dreamed of for so long, but also a day that I wasn't sure would ever truly arrive. As I lay there for a moment, trying to shake the sleep from my body, a flood of emotions began to wash over me. Today wasn't just another match day; today was the day that Sam and I would visit ground No. 42 out of 42 of the SPFL clubs. It was the day our journey – one that started as an idea, then transformed into a goal and eventually an all-consuming mission – would finally come full circle.

I sat up in bed, letting the weight of the moment sink in. For years, this had felt like a distant dream. I had no idea where this journey would take me when it first began. It was never really about ticking off boxes or simply visiting stadiums for the sake of it. It was about so much more: the people I met, the stories I gathered, the way Scottish football in all its imperfections and brilliance, became intertwined with my own life and my journey with Sam. If I'm being honest, there were times I doubted if I'd reach the finish line. Life has a way of throwing curveballs at you, and over the years, I'd faced more than my fair share. Yet, here we were, on the brink of completing something truly special.

Sam came wandering through to my bedroom, as he does every morning when he hears my alarm, completely unaware of the significance of the day ahead. He was calm, as always. His steady presence had been my constant companion throughout this entire adventure. I often wondered what he thought of it all, the train journeys, the stadiums, the cheers and the chants. While I navigated the highs and lows of football fandom, Sam was there for the journey, patiently guiding me through packed concourses, up narrow stairways and into stands that hummed with the energy of match day. Today would be no different, except that it marked the culmination of something much bigger than a single game.

The attention now following us online meant what began as a personal mission for Sam and me had grown into something much bigger. After capturing the interest of supporters on social media, it also made its way into the mainstream media. I never set out for any recognition, but as the weeks and months passed, it became clear that what we were doing had struck a chord with people. It wasn't just about football, it was about resilience, determination and showing that accessibility in sport was a cause worth fighting for.

What surprised me most, though, was when the SPFL themselves got in touch. A few months before we were set to visit our final ground, I received an email, and I remember reading it with a mixture of disbelief and excitement. They had heard about our journey and wanted to play a part. They wanted to join us for that final match, to film a video about our story for their YouTube and other social media channels, and to put out a press release celebrating the milestone. I was blown away. For an organisation like the SPFL to notice what we were doing, and then to actively want to help us share it with the wider football community, felt like a huge honour. All the long journeys, the challenges and the moments of doubt now felt worth it.

Naturally, I didn't hesitate to agree. How could I? To have the SPFL's backing was a validation of everything Sam and I had worked towards. Their support was a reminder that accessibility in football was finally getting the attention it deserved. I was eager to meet Molly and Gregor from the SPFL, who had been coordinating the logistics. We arranged to meet them at Station Park in Forfar on the day of the game, and I couldn't wait to share that final moment as they documented the conclusion of our epic journey.

But the media interest didn't stop there. In the week leading up to that final match, the production company behind *A View from the Terrace*, the popular BBC Scotland TV show, reached out. They wanted to do a feature on me and Sam for an upcoming episode. I was stunned. I had watched the show myself many times, and I knew how much it meant to Scottish football fans. To have them reach out and say they wanted to film an interview about our journey was another moment that felt unreal. Again, I was more than happy to oblige.

The crew from *A View from the Terrace* planned to arrive at my home around 9.00 a.m. on the morning of the game. They wanted to capture not just the final match but also the story of the day leading up to it, the moment when Sam was about to make Scottish football history. When they pulled up that morning, cameras and equipment in tow, it hit me just how far we had come. What had started as a personal goal, something I'd set out to do for myself, had become a story that people wanted to share with others. It was humbling, and in that moment, I felt a mix of pride and disbelief.

The filming was intimate, much more than I had expected. As they asked questions, I found myself reflecting on the entire journey: our experiences at the other 41 grounds, the laughter, the challenges, and the sheer joy of visiting each ground with Sam by my side. I spoke about the moments that had stuck with me, the people I'd met along the way and the unforgettable memories we'd created. There was a sense of emotion in recounting it all, knowing that it was now reaching its conclusion.

Once the interview was wrapped up, the film crew packed their gear and we then made our way to Forfar. Arriving at Station Park later that day, with Molly and Gregor from the SPFL waiting for us, I felt the weight of the moment. This was it, No. 42. And as the cameras rolled, capturing every step Sam and I took, I couldn't help but think of how far we had come, not just in distance but in everything we had achieved. It wasn't just a journey across football grounds, it was a journey that had touched the hearts of so many. And now, with the SPFL and *A View from the Terrace* there to celebrate it with us, it felt like we had truly made a lasting impact on Scottish football.

Sam and I arrived at Station Park around an hour and a half before kick-off. This was to give us enough time to do some filming with Molly and Gregor from the SPFL

– shots of us arriving at Station Park, inside the ground and heading up to our seats in the main stand. They also filmed a short interview about why I decided to take on this challenge and about the amazing support we had gained along the way. The film crew from *A View from the Terrace* were also filming some footage at the game for their piece as well.

As well as the SPFL team and the crew from *A View from the Terrace*, this day was going to be a special gathering of friends and supporters who had been part of our journey. One of the first people to confirm they would be there was my good friend Nigel, who made the long drive up from Carlisle to Forfar to be with us. His dedication in making the trip just reinforced how important these moments were, not only for me but for the people around me who had shared in the experience.

I was also thrilled that Moira, Dundee United's Disability Access Officer, was able to join us. She has been a key figure in helping me navigate accessibility challenges over the years, particularly at Tannadice. Her work has made such a difference for disabled supporters at Dundee United, ensuring that everyone has the chance to enjoy the game on equal footing. To have her there, not only as a supporter but as someone who has contributed so much to improving accessibility in Scottish football, was a real honour. Her presence felt symbolic of the wider cause Sam and I were championing, a reminder of how many people are working hard behind the scenes to make football more inclusive for all.

Another familiar face who made the journey to Station Park was Stuart, one of the audio-descriptive commentators from Dundee United. Stuart had been providing the audio commentary for me at Tannadice for years, helping me and many others on a match day at Tannadice stay connected to the game in a way that would otherwise be difficult. His commentary had become such a valuable part of my experience, and having him there to provide the same service for the match was incredible. It was almost like a personal touch, a piece of Tannadice coming with me to the final ground.

Stuart's commentary wasn't just for my benefit that day, though. The SPFL and *A View From The Terrace* were both recording his audio feed to highlight how crucial these kinds of services are for visually impaired supporters as part of their video package they were both putting together. The fact that they wanted to showcase this service in their coverage of our story was deeply moving. It wasn't just about me and Sam anymore, it was about raising awareness for the accessibility options that make football more enjoyable for so many. The audio-descriptive commentary is one of those services that often goes unnoticed unless you need it, but for those of us who do, it makes all the difference in the world. To know that this moment would help shine a light on the importance of such services made me really proud.

The day was shaping up to be a true celebration, of completing the 42 grounds and of everything that the journey stood for – friendship, accessibility and the shared passion for football that brings people together. Everyone who joined us, from Nigel to Moira to Stuart, had played a part in making this day possible, and their presence added layers of meaning to an already momentous occasion. This was going to be a day I'd never forget, made even more special by the people who chose to be there by our side.

The final whistle blew, and Forfar Athletic secured a 2-1 victory. As the cheers and applause echoed around Station

Park, a wave of emotion swept over me. This was it: Sam and I had finally completed our mission! We had visited and watched a live game at all 42 SPFL football grounds. It was a moment I had dreamed of but wasn't sure would ever happen, and now, standing there with Sam by my side, it was a reality. It felt unreal, like the culmination of years of effort, dedication, thousands of miles travelled and unforgettable memories had all come together in this one, fleeting moment.

As the players left the pitch and the crowd began to disperse, I thought that would be the end. But then, the SPFL had one more surprise in store. As I gathered my things, I was approached by a member of the SPFL staff, who told me they had a special presentation to make. They invited Sam and me onto the pitch at Station Park, something I hadn't expected at all. Walking out onto the field where so many had celebrated victories and suffered defeats, I couldn't help but feel overwhelmed by the significance of the moment.

Standing there on the pitch, the SPFL team presented us with something that took my breath away, a Special Recognition Award. The feeling of being honoured in such a way, on that very ground, was beyond words. They handed me an official SPFL Special Recognition award, but what really brought a tear to my eye was when they presented Sam with his very own SPFL special recognition medal. Sam, my loyal companion through this incredible journey, was being celebrated alongside me. He had earned it just as much, if not more, than I had. After all, Sam wasn't just any dog, he had just made Scottish football history. He had become the first dog ever to visit all 42 SPFL grounds.

Seeing Sam proudly wearing his medal was one of those moments I'll cherish forever. Every mile we travelled, every challenge we faced, and every game we attended had led us to this point. The medal was a testament to the bond Sam and I shared and the perseverance we had shown.

This official recognition meant the world to me. Not just because it marked the end of an incredible journey, but because it showed that what Sam and I had achieved resonated with others too. It was more than a personal victory; it was something bigger, something that had touched the hearts of football fans and beyond. As I stood there on the pitch, I thought about all the people who had followed our journey, the messages of support we had received, and the community that had gathered.

This wasn't just my story, it was Sam's story, and it was the story of everyone who had been there with us along the way.

The day after we completed the 42, the SPFL put out a press release to news outlets about mine and Sam's incredible achievement. The release included pictures from the day, photos of us both standing proudly on the pitch at Station Park, Sam with his medal and me with my award. The SPFL also released the video they had filmed, capturing the emotion and significance of the day, and posted it across their social media channels. The response was overwhelming in the best possible way. The football community – fans, clubs and even players – embraced our story with open arms, flooding social media with messages of congratulations and support. I was humbled by how far our journey had reached.

What followed was a whirlwind of press opportunities that I never could have imagined. We were invited to BBC

Scotland's studios in Glasgow to appear on *The Nine*, where Sam charmed everyone he met. BBC 5 Live, Tay FM and Clyde 1 *Superscoreboard* reached out for interviews, and we even found ourselves recording podcast episodes, including one for the BBC Scottish Football Podcast. It seemed that wherever I turned, someone was eager to hear about our journey, our experiences and, more importantly, the cause that had driven us from day one: promoting accessibility in football.

Print media got in on the action too. Newspapers and magazines printed stories, all sparked from the SPFL's press release. Seeing our journey written about in publications I had grown up reading was unreal. But what struck me most was how these outlets framed our story, not just as a personal triumph but as a step forward in the ongoing conversation about accessibility in football. It was clear that what Sam and I had, in our own small way, brought the conversation about accessibility in Scottish football to the forefront.

The weeks that followed were a blur of media attention, interviews and congratulations from people across the country. It was overwhelming, but in the best way possible. I hadn't expected any of it – the widespread media coverage, the messages of support, the way our journey resonated with so many people. But the most touching part was knowing that we had started important conversations, conversations that might lead to real change.

As I sit here, reflecting on everything Sam and I have been through together, I realise that this journey has been about more than just football or even accessibility. It's been about community, connection and the unbreakable bond between a man and his guide dog. It's about every person who supported us, every club that welcomed us, and every challenge we overcame along the way.

This experience will live with me for the rest of my life. Not just because we completed the 42, but because of what that journey represents: hope, resilience, and the belief that with enough determination, change is possible. And if our story helps even one person feel more included, more heard or more understood, then every step we took, every game we attended, was worth it.

Sam and I set out on this journey to complete all 42 SPFL grounds, but what we achieved went beyond even our wildest dreams. We brought accessibility to the forefront of the conversation in Scottish football – and that, more than anything, is the legacy I hope will endure.

EPILOGUE

It's early morning, and the world outside is still quiet. Sam is curled up beside me, his gentle breathing a comforting presence as I sip my first cup of coffee of the day. The thought hits me: today is just another day, but it's also a day that signifies the end of a journey I could never have imagined when it first began. Sam and I have visited the grounds of all 42 Scottish Professional Football League clubs, a feat that seemed impossible at times. It's a story of passion, perseverance and the unbreakable bond between a man and his guide dog.

It's been about a month since Sam and I completed our journey, and life has taken on a strange kind of normality again. As I sit here, reflecting on everything we've accomplished, I can't help but feel a deep sense of gratitude, not just for the journey itself but for the people, places and moments that shaped it.

When we set out to complete the 42, I never anticipated how much our story would resonate with others. Sure, I knew it would be a personal challenge, a way to marry my love of football with the desire to push the boundaries of what's possible as a visually impaired person. But I didn't expect the widespread interest, the media attention or the emotional connections we would form with fellow fans, clubs and even the SPFL. It's been overwhelming, in the most amazing way.

Sam, of course, has taken it all in his stride. As a guide dog, his world is one of focus, purpose and loyalty. He doesn't know, or care, that he's now something of a Scottish football celebrity. To him, he's just doing what he does best: keeping me safe, guiding me through the chaos of crowds, and offering companionship that's so much more than words can ever express. But to everyone else, he's a trailblazer, a history maker, the first dog to visit all 42 grounds and a symbol of what can be achieved when we break down barriers.

The weeks following our completion of the quest were a whirlwind. I still remember the flood of press requests that came in after the SPFL put out their press release about our achievement. Each interview was a chance to tell our story, to highlight not only our love for the game but also the broader message about accessibility and inclusion in football.

The support we received was staggering. Social media was ablaze with messages from football fans across the country, congratulating us and sharing their own experiences of the game. Some of them were fellow disabled fans, who spoke about the challenges they faced in attending matches, the lack of accessible seating, the difficulties in navigating older stadiums, the frustration of being overlooked by clubs. Others were simply fans who had followed our journey and were inspired by what Sam and I had achieved.

But while the media coverage and public recognition were incredible, they were never the reason we did this. For me, the heart of this journey has always been about the love of the game. Football has been a constant in my life, through the highs and lows, the victories and defeats, the moments of pure joy and crushing disappointment. It's been a way to connect with others, to feel part of something bigger than myself, even when life has thrown its toughest challenges my way.

In many ways, football is a metaphor for life itself. There are times when everything goes your way, when the ball hits the back of the net and the crowd erupts in celebration. But there are also times when things don't go as planned, when you're faced with obstacles that seem insurmountable. As a visually impaired person, I've had my share of those moments. But if this journey has taught me anything, it's that resilience, determination and a little bit of faith can carry you through even the toughest of times.

Sam, of course, has been my rock throughout it all. His steady presence, his unwavering loyalty and his unspoken understanding have made this journey possible. I couldn't have done any of this without him. And while he may not understand the magnitude of what we've accomplished together, I know that he's played a vital role in making it happen.

As we crossed the final finish line, there was a feeling of bittersweet satisfaction. We had completed what we set out to do, and yet, I couldn't help but wonder what comes next. How do you follow up on something as monumental as visiting all 42 SPFL grounds? For a while, I wasn't sure. But then, as the dust began to settle, I realised that this journey wasn't really the end, it was just the beginning.

The conversation about accessibility in football is far from over. There is still so much work to be done, both in Scotland and beyond, to ensure that disabled fans have equal access to the game we all love. And that's where my focus is now, continuing to advocate for change, working with clubs, supporters' associations, and organisations like Level Playing Field and AccessibAll to push for better facilities, more inclusive policies and greater awareness of the challenges faced by disabled fans.

One of the things I've learned through this journey is that change doesn't happen overnight. It takes time, effort and persistence. But it also takes people who are willing to speak up, to challenge the status quo and to demand better. That's what Sam and I have tried to do, and it's what I will continue to do in the future.

As I close this chapter of our lives, I'm filled with a sense of optimism for what the future holds. Our journey may be over, but the impact of what we've done will continue to ripple through Scottish football for years to come. We've started a conversation, and now it's up to all of us – fans, clubs, players and organisations – to keep that conversation going.

Football has always been a game of passion, but it's also a game of inclusivity. It brings people together from all walks of life, united by a common love for the sport. And if there's one thing I've learned from this experience, it's that football truly has the power to change the world.

* * *

As I finish writing these final words, Sam is very sadly no longer by my side. On Sunday, 16 March, 2025 Sam very suddenly and unexpectedly passed away. He was only 8 years old.

I am utterly devastated and heartbroken by the loss of my guide and, more importantly, my best friend of almost 7 years. There are no words to describe the pain I feel.

However, I take comfort in seeing how well loved he was by everyone in Scottish football. Sam touched the hearts of many football fans across the country and will forever hold a unique place in Scottish football history.

Together, we completed an extraordinary journey, one that has taken us to every corner of Scotland and beyond. But as I look to the future, as hard as it seems now, I know that there are still new adventures waiting for me, new challenges to face, new grounds to visit and new conversations to be had.

This is not the end.

My journey continues.

THE 42 GROUNDS

Ground No. 1 Dens Park – Dundee

Ground No. 2 McDiarmid Park – St Johnstone

Ground No. 3 Firhill Stadium – Partick Thistle

Ground No. 4 Pittodrie Stadium – Aberdeen

Ground No. 5 New Central Park – Kelty Hearts

Ground No. 6 Ibrox – Rangers

Ground No. 7 Victoria Park – Ross County

Ground No. 8 Easter Road – Hibernian

Ground No. 9 Gayfield – Arbroath

Ground No. 10 Somerset Park – Ayr United

Ground No. 11 Caledonian Stadium – Inverness Caledonian Thistle

Ground Nos. 12 and 13 New Douglas Park – Clyde and Hamilton Academical

Ground No. 14 Tynecastle Park – Heart of Midlothian

Ground No. 15 Hampden Park – Queen's Park

Ground No. 16 Cappielow Park – Greenock Morton

Ground No. 17 Meadowbank Stadium – Edinburgh City

Ground No. 18 Galabank – Annan Athletic

Ground No. 19 Ochilview Park – Stenhousemuir

Ground No. 20 Albert Bartlett Stadium – Airdrieonians

Ground No. 21 Borough Briggs – Elgin City

Ground No. 22 Ainslie Park – Spartans

Ground No. 23 Indodrill Stadium – Alloa Athletic

Ground No. 24 Forthbank Stadium – Stirling Albion

Ground No. 25 Stark's Park – Raith Rovers

Ground No. 26 Stair Park – Stranraer

Ground No. 27 Tony Macaroni Arena – Livingston

Ground No. 28 The Rock – Dumbarton

Ground No. 29 Balmoral Stadium – Cove Rangers

Ground No. 30 Fir Park – Motherwell

Ground No. 31 Falkirk Stadium – Falkirk

Ground No. 32 East End Park – Dunfermline Athletic

Ground No. 33 Balmoor Stadium – Peterhead

Ground No. 34 Bayview Stadium – East Fife

Ground No. 35 Rugby Park – Kilmarnock

Ground No. 36 New Dundas Park – Bonnyrigg Rose

Ground No. 37 Links Park – Montrose

Ground No. 38 Palmerston Park – Queen of the South

Ground No. 39 SMISA Stadium – St Mirren

Ground No. 40 Celtic Park – Celtic

Ground No. 41 Tannadice Park - Dundee United

Ground No. 42 Station Park – Forfar

ABOUT THE AUTHOR

Jon Attenborough, from Perth in Scotland, is registered blind and a dedicated advocate for accessibility and inclusivity. Jon brings a unique perspective to his work with a mission to make sports more accessible for everyone. His expertise is around disability access to football, and he has worked with clubs in Scotland and the Premier League highlighting the importance of inclusivity in sports and society. Between Twitter (X) and TikTok Jon has a highly engaged audience. Jon has also made various mainstream media appearances with BBC and STV News and has also appeared on many podcasts.

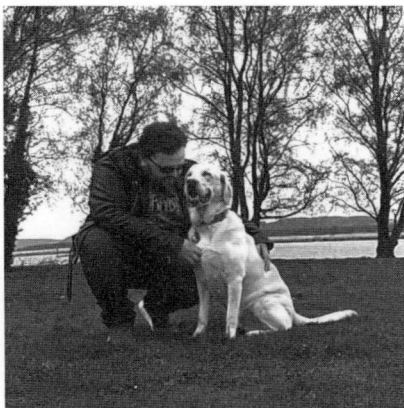

ACKNOWLEDGEMENTS

Thank you so much to everyone who has supported me and Sam's incredible journey. Thank you to the SPFL for going out of the way to recognise and commemorate our achievement. Thank you to all 42 SPFL clubs who welcomed me and Sam to your grounds with open arms. Finally, thank you also to McNidder & Grace for believing in our story and allowing me to share it in this book with all of you.

REST IN PEACE SAM

2016-2025

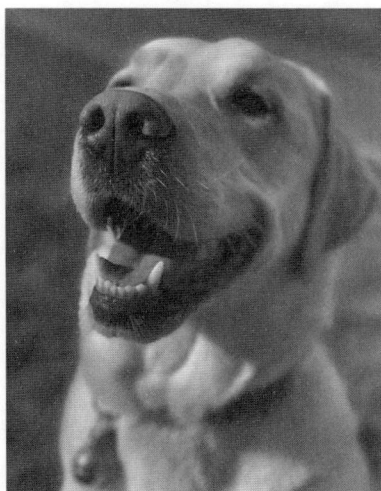

Thank you Sam for the life you have enabled me to live. Without you, completing this extraordinary journey would not have been possible. You have been my constant companion and best friend and life won't be the same without you.

Love you, Sam. Rest easy my friend.